Couch Potatoes Sprout

The Rise of Online Community Journalism

Jack Driscoll

To order additional copies of this book, contact:
Xlibris Corporation
1-888-795-4274
www.Xlibris.com
Orders@Xlibris.com
51933

Couch Potatoes Sprout

Contents

Dedication

I wish to dedicate this book to reporters of every variety.
Their role is more vital to democracy than ever.

INTRODUCTION

*"Buzz is no longer two people at a cocktail party;
now anybody with a computer is a newspaper."*

**Chris Pula, Warner Brothers,
in Variety Magazine, July 28, 1997**

THEY HAD NO idea what they were getting into. "We want to be on the cutting edge," she said, and nine heads nodded in agreement. That was in the Spring of 1996, when few knew what the internet was and even fewer understood what a website was, including these ten senior citizens. Nevertheless that's exactly what they were agreeing to take on: A website.

Thus began what may be the longest-publishing citizens group in existence at a city senior center in a converted carriage house in Melrose, Mass., 10 miles north of Boston. They call themselves the SilverStringers, and their monthly publication is entitled The Melrose Mirror.

Now, more than a decade later a digital phenomenon known as "citizen journalism" is beginning to heat up.

Blogging is the most identifiable form. But the term "citizen journalism" also conjures up images of the live coverage of the Indonesian tsunami and Hurricane Katrina, as non-professionals using cellphone photos and digital video captured the enormity of the events.

Less dramatic but a steadily growing piece of the pie is group-generated community journalism, stepping to the fore at a time when traditional media is retreating, trimming news personnel and leaving gaps in local and specialty reporting. So far groups have generally operated in geographical areas, but the inevitability of community-of-interest groups with members spread nationally or worldwide will bring an added dimension to the movement.

This book explores the concept of community group journalism and explains how it is done.

The book zeroes in on the inside workings of three grassroots groups that, combined, have rolled up a total of more than 20 years of operation. Two are community publishing entities and one was run by children and teenagers from around the world. The aim is to provide insight into a quiet revolution by a new breed of communicators who are taking advantage of new electronic tools that enable their voices to be heard from here (wherever they are) to Timbuktu (literally).

Essentially these new journalists are learning by doing with an enthusiasm that is contagious. The emphasis in this book will be more on the "how" than on the "who, what, when, where and why". Tutorials on the various levels of publishing for others who "want to be on the cutting edge" also will be included in these pages. The tutorials, geared for understanding by teens and adults, are based on my good fortune of having had a foot in both the old media (44 years) and new media camps (more than 15 years).

The three groups are:

The Melrose Mirror SilverStringers: The "cutting edge" comment grew out of a meeting among inquisitive seniors and representatives of the MIT Media Laboratory in 1996. A variety of ideas for collaboration were thrown out for discussion, but the publishing possibility seemed to stick with the volunteers who attended. Oddly, only two of the ten had computers – and neither computer was connected to the internet. Experience? One had done some writing, photography and ad selling for the local weekly, and another had done some freelance review writing. The rest were novices. A couple of months after the first meeting, in June of 1996, the site was born, becoming a model within a year for other sites nearby as well as in Finland, Thailand, Italy, Ireland, Brazil, India and elsewhere. About 20 Melrose regulars, who meet weekly, anchor the site, handling reporting, writing, photography and technical aspects. For a couple of years they had the advantage of twice-a-month, one-hour instruction sessions by Media Lab students and staff, one session dealing with technology and the other with journalism. Quickly they became evangelists, helping three communities within a short distance start up and even sending a delegation to Ennis, Ireland, for a week of workshops that led to a senior website there three months later. Publishing 15 to 20 stories each month, the SilverStringers provide features, some news, travel pieces, poetry, recipes and special projects, such as The Great Depression, World War II and Victorian Homes in the community. The Depression package led to a 26-chapter book by an 87-year-old member, Bill Jodrey, who had been a hobo. Meanwhile, another early member, Marjorie Burgess, then in her 80s, wrote a theme song for the site. A published music composer, Burgess called the song

"The Kangaroo Troop", because "the notes go up and down." (Both Jodrey and Burgess are deceased). The Melrose Mirror is well-known for its photographs. A team of 5 or 6 goes out regularly and shoots a couple of hundred photographs at a pre-determined locale, then they pick the best for a photo essay. More than 100 individuals have been regulars or contributors to the Melrose Mirror. In 2007 three SilverStringers ran a workshop at the AARP national convention on citizen journalism. (The name "SilverStringers" was coined by Steve Newhouse, CEO of AdvanceNet; the URL for their site is *http://melrosemirror.media.mit.edu*).

Joint meeting of Melrose, Rye groups. (Photo by SilverStringer Don Norris)

The Junior Journal: Curiosity and the power of positive thinking created this remarkable global monthly literally overnight. Starting with members between ages 10 and 16 and later extending the age limit to 18, the Junior Journal had more than 300 participants from 91 countries over a period of seven years – and some editions carried as many as 70 stories. The Junior Journal began in 1998 – modeled after the SilverStringers and using the same software – and was discontinued in 2005, not because of a lack of personnel or enthusiasm, but because the editors all went off to college. The "JJ", as they called it, started with 12 editors, one for each month. They rejected the concept of an "editor-in-chief". They also rejected any adult involvement, except for occasionally tapping into the experience of an adult adviser (yours truly). Communication was entirely by email, often at the rate of 100 per day, as they suggested and planned stories, argued over a variety of issues and somehow came to consensus. The Journal was a spin-off of the 1998 Junior Summit. They wrote about major children's issues (child labor, child soldiers, AIDs, discrimination, etc.) and major world issues (Mideast turmoil, the Gulf War, environment, poverty, etc.), and they poured out features to help explain the customs and cultures of their countries. As a matter of policy, they wrote almost all their stories in English, even though it was a second language for most, because they felt English was the most widely read language. They won the only contest they entered, the Global Junior Challenge, and sent an editor to Rome to receive the trophy. (The URL for the site that has archives of seven years of stories is http://journal.jrsmmit.net).

Spiros Tzelepis of Greece, who started as an editor at age 12, received Global Junior Award in Rome on behalf of Junior Journal.

The Rye Reflections Surfers: Could a citizen website sustain itself in a quiet seaside town with a population of only 5200? Started in Rye, N.H., in June, 2005, Rye Reflections took hold rapidly. Again the Melrose Mirror was the model, and a half dozen SilverStringers drove 45 miles to the adjoining state to help at one of the organizing meetings. Rye also was chosen, partly because it is where I live. Meetings started three months before the first issue. Only four citizens showed up for the first two meetings, but word-of-mouth attracted six or eight more by June when the first issue was published. Within a year there were 15 regulars (those who attended the weekly meetings) and a half-dozen frequent contributors. Melrose and Rye are similar but differ. They use the same software, publish monthly and lean heavily on photography. But Rye is more news-oriented, extends its coverage to surrounding seacoast communities and has had contributors who range in age from 14 to 99. The "Rye Surfers", as they call themselves, meet in the Rye Public Library. Coverage of three major coastal storms in the first two years of existence raised Rye Reflections' profile, as did ongoing coverage of a controversial police-fire building project that took two years to complete instead of the planned one year. Like the Melrose Stringers, the Surfers have had hardly any background in journalism, didn't know one another in most cases before joining and represent a kaleidoscope of careers from airline hostess to banker to teacher to ski slope operator to engineer to CIA employee to auto dealer. "Rye Crisp", a news tidbits column that all contribute to, consistently comes out tops in monthly readership based on Stat Counter and Google Analytics. The site was graced by the features and poetry of well-known summer resident Polly Morton, who died in 2008. When her first of dozens of articles appeared in July, 2005, she was 97 years old. (The URL is *http://ryereflections.org*).

Mainstream Media Sideswiped

The stories behind the stories that have flowed from these three citizen-journalism groups as described in subsequent chapters will reflect what it is like in the trenches and what can be forecast about the future of community journalism. How are groups started? How do they organize? What policies do they have to come to grips with? What tricky issues do they face? How do they sustain themselves? Who does what and how? What tools do they have to have and what tools can make life easier? Why do they do it?

The rise of citizen journalism has been spawned by the invention of the Worldwide Web while being abetted by the mainstream media's drift toward a fixation with the bottom line and away from its responsibilities as servant of the public.

Little did anyone know that the dynamics of all forms of communications would change so dramatically at the turn of this century as the internet began to blossom.[1]

With the exception of telephone, which had certain limitations, the essential forms of print and electronic communication went in one direction: Piped from the media to its audience. The internet is a two-way street.

The mainstream media in all its facets has been sideswiped from two directions. On the one hand its audiences are relying less and less on newspapers, radio and television, partly because they can get their information elsewhere, usually faster and at a low cost, and partly because time spent online is reducing time spent with the major media. With the shift in readership and viewership goes a shift in advertising dollars.

How will these two worlds look twenty years from now? Will they co-exist, merge somehow or will one of them fall by the wayside?

Through the close-up prism of the three groups and their spin-offs being described in this book, some hints as to the future of community journalism will emerge. Clearly newspapers are staring down the barrel of a musket as the digital shift shreds 250 years of operating by essentially the same rulebook. For citizen journalism, on the other hand, the best is yet to come.

"Historians will look back on our times, the 40-year span between 1980 and 2020, and classify it among the handful of historical moments when humans reorganized their civilization around a new tool, a new idea . . ." wrote Peter Leyden, managing editor of Wired, in 1998.[2]

Flood at Rye horse farm (Photo by Judy Underwood)

CHAPTER ONE

Information Disruption

"The only free press belongs to those who own one."

– Mark Twain

THE DIGITAL REVOLUTION has opened the doors to new voices, new ideas, new perspectives – and new opportunities for all citizens. No longer do you need to own a printing press or a broadcast channel to have your voice heard. No longer is the average person just a receptor of information. The consumer is now a creator. The ability to communicate widely and at little cost through words, voices or images is at everyone's fingertips.

Within the revolution is an evolution. In the beginning, quickly out of the box, came one-to-one email and one-to-many email followed by chat, then blogging, podcasting and videocasting. Now, lumbering along and only recently picking up steam is the group-publishing form of citizen journalism.

More and more individuals and groups are discovering that citizen journalism is empowering; it provides a responsible outlet for strongly-held views; it creates connections among like-minded communities; it awakens a realization that average citizens have the ability and means of communicating locally and even globally in a way that previously was out of reach, largely available only to professionals. This movement is more than a pendulum swing; it is a disruption in an information process that had been one way and now, because of the internet, is flowing from multiple points to and from multiple points simultaneously. From centralized to decentralized in the blink of an eye.

At the grassroots level the realization of this new-found ability to be part of the dialogue at all levels, be it local or global, is just beginning to dawn. It's one thing to understand that new tools of communication are now available to you; it's another to come to grips with the fact that those tools are becoming easier and easier to use, and you don't have to have special expertise to be part of the dialogue. Being a member of a group helps break down preconceptions and provides a comfortable setting for learning. The act of putting the toe into the water seems to be the biggest hurdle for so-called average citizens.

The Energizing Effect

These conclusions are more than academic. They are based on the experiences of three groups in particular and numerous other citizen journalists who have already tasted the fruits of publishing satisfaction.

The Melrose Mirror, the Junior Journal and Rye Reflections are all non-profits (numerous community group sites have gone the for-profit route). The members are motivated by dual desires: public service and personal satisfaction.

No one has been more surprised at their successes than the participants themselves. They have learned to write by writing. They have been so motivated to publish that many, who didn't even know what the word meant, have even learned programming. Me included. And they have developed a keener appreciation of what the mainstream media faces.

Still, all three groups have rejected the top-down approach that works in the professional world. These young and old citizen groups seem to function best as social organizations. Power is shared and rotated. Decisions are not made by fiat but by consensus.

Group journalism is culturally compatible with the Open Source movement, best known for use by software developers. As described in Wikipedia, "The open source model of operation and decision making allows concurrent input of different agendas, approaches and priorities, and differs from the more closed, centralized models of development."

Journalism-by-groups is likely to be the next big thing in citizen journalism. It is further proof that two heads are better than one. Ideas are distilled and shaped by a variety of experiences, expertise and perspectives. Some participants see ideas in words, others in visual forms such as artwork or photos or video. Get them working together, and you have the best of all communication worlds.

Jim Cerny was visiting a friend in Portsmouth, N.H., had his camera with him (as usual) and caught this hawk on a telephone line waiting to pounce on a backyard pet.

Standing back and surveying this new phenomenon, two aspects are evident:

- The energizing effect that participation in the new media has on those involved.
- The new definition of news that is evolving as more and more diverse groups pop up around the world.

These are two themes – social networking and citizen news – that will be looked at in more depth in the course of this book. A quick comment on the energizing effect: The stimulation, the fulfillment and the fun that flow from this new-found process among young and old are readily apparent.

A Melrose woman returned from her first interview at a local coffee shop and was asked by the group how it went. "I feel like I am 35 again," she bubbled. (We don't divulge women's ages, so let's just say she pretty much cut her actual years in half.)

Medical research relating to active seniors versus "couch potatoes" shows that an engaged person generally will live longer because of the effect that mental, physical and social activity have on brain cells. More on this later as well.

Public's Right & Responsibility

Youngsters working in community experience a similar uplift: They're learning from their experiences, they're developing relationships on a healthy plane, they're contributing to a society that often frustrates them and frequently ignores them. Their voices are being heard, and more often than not they have something significant to say.

No matter what age, many are still trying to make the adjustment to this new-media world. After years of being served breakfast in bed, it's hard to get up and make your own meal. In effect the public has been fairly satisfied with a system in which news is served on a platter.

"Freedom of the Press" has been seen as a right accorded to professionals, but the First Amendment, an offshoot of European bills of rights, was aimed more at protecting individual rights. Among those rights were any expression spoken or in print. Pamphlets, a pre-cursor to civic-journalism publications, were a prevalent mode of written expression during the early debates on rights issues.

Most professional journalists rightfully see themselves as representing the public, being eyes and ears; thus acting on the public's behalf. As a veteran criminal justice reporter for the Boston Herald and Boston Globe, Richard Connolly frequently sought out records at government offices and courthouses. Good reporters rely on public records. He would always say, "My name is Richard Connolly, and I would like records regarding . . ." He never mentioned that he was working for a news organization.

Connolly contended that each time he asked for a record, he was reinforcing the public's right to such access.

Somehow the media managers have lost their focus on such principles.

- Public-servant idealism remains strong among reporters at the "street level" but seems to dissipate at higher levels in news organizations where bottom-line concerns more and more outweigh concerns for the public interest.
- Print and broadcast newsrooms are cutting back on reporters to keep budgets in check.
- The number of news outlets is diminishing.
- News websites are replete with wire-service stories, because these websites rarely have any writers and/or reporters of their own.
- Network television viewership is off by about a third, radio listening is at an all-time low and newspaper circulation has been trending downward for almost 20 years.
- Corporatization, particularly in the print media, has diminished concern for the community. Family-owned newspapers are fast fading.

In a speech on Sept. 11, 2004, Bill Moyers said: "The framers of our nation never envisioned these huge media giants . . . never imagined what could happen if big government, big publishing and big broadcasters ever saw eye to eye in putting the public's need for news second to their own interests." What's fascinating – and encouraging – is that in this era of drastic staff reductions, a proliferation of new voices and new insights are being seen and heard around the world.

Broadened Definition of News

If a tree falls in the forest and there's no reporter around to take note, did it happen? If there aren't enough reporters to cover traditional news events, such as local government or school meetings, how does the public find out what's going on? Can citizen journalists help fill some of the void? What is news anyway? Or another way of putting it: Can the citizens' news be defined any longer without direct input from the citizens?

Those who have labored in the media vineyards know that news is more than event coverage. News deals with information of a timely nature about events, people, issues and trends that are significant or of interest to the audience. Network anchorman John Chancellor used to describe news as "a chronicle of conflict and change."

The late Prof. James Carey, in his days as communications dean at the University of Illinois and later as a professor at Columbia University's graduate school, delved more deeply into the definition in a provocative book called, "Communication as Culture": "News reading, and writing, is a ritual act and moreover a dramatic one. What is arrayed before the reader is not pure information but a portrayal of the contending forces in the world. Moreover, as readers make their way through the paper, they engage in a continual shift of roles or of dramatic focus . . . news is not information but drama. It does not describe the world but portrays an arena of dramatic forces and action; it exists solely in historical time; and it invites our participation on the basis of our assuming, often vicariously, social roles within it."

What does that say to those who are involved or will become involved in community journalism? First, it says that community journalists have something to say that is beneficial to readers; second, they are qualified to do so.

Groupthink Pays Dividends

What citizen journalists have to say results from their special knowledge of their community. Partly that knowledge comes under the heading of accumulated and shared wisdom among these community journalists. Partly it comes from knowing what's going on in their own environs.

Here's a concrete example:

Most cities and towns are built near rivers or lakes or ponds. In the center of Melrose is Ell Pond, a picturesque spot that belies the pollution that closed it to swimming more than a half century ago. Ell Pond was the natural subject for a story on the SilverStringers' website, so an editor raised the issue at one of their weekly meetings with about 15 participants sitting around a conference table. "Why don't we do a story on Ell Pond? It's the centerpiece of our town. Who wants to work on it?"

"I'll call the Parks and Recreation director and find out if they ever plan to open it again for swimming." "Someone should contact the Army Corps of Engineers. They once wanted to install some sort of rappelling along one side of it." "Another source of information is the abutters. They formed an association to preserve the pond." "We also should talk to some of the people who used to swim down there before it closed. When was it, early Forties?" "I used to swim there. I can tell you all about the bloodsuckers. Yyyech." "My father was the ticket-taker at the little public beach. He's got a million stories." And so it went. Would a metropolitan newspaper planning the same story be able to tap into the same wisdom in a few minutes? It's likely that even a local weekly would lack such perspective without taking the time for a lot of interviews. Time they don't have. Costs too much. A trained reporter, of course, would understand the need to interview certain individuals and follow certain threads. And the professional would know to check records and library references and might have expertise in environmental matters. That reporter might also see the story in the broader context of other ponds in the community or state.

Still, the community person has his or her own set of qualifications that could be considered unique (except that my first real Editor, Laurence L. Winship of the Boston Globe banned the word "unique" on the basis that there is no such thing in this world). What's most lacking at the community level is self-assurance. Citizens have trouble envisioning themselves as writers or broadcasters. They are fast learning.

Aquarian Conspirators

The grassroots genie was out of the bottle even before the internet took hold. Author Marilyn Ferguson described the powerful political and social transformations that she said were changing the world's culture in her 1980 book "Aquarian Conspiracy". She described how like-minded individuals, uninhibited by distance, were forming networks that are bringing about radical change. "It is a conspiracy without political doctrine. Without a manifesto. With conspirators who seek power only to disperse it . . . Activists asking different kinds of questions, challenging the establishment from within."

Sounds like citizen journalists.

Ferguson took her transformation theory one step further when she wrote, " . . . the conspirators are linked, made kindred by their inner discoveries and earthquakes. You can break through old limits, past inertia and fear, to levels of fulfillment that once seemed impossible . . . (Conspirators) are at once antennae and transmitters, both listening and communicating."

Ferguson's foresight seems to have drawn a roadmap for community journalists that calls not only for the coming together in transformative groups but also the creating of links between and among groups to help share, sustain and strengthen one another. Sort of an association of community journalist groups devoted to self-nurturing.

Technologists already are exploiting the potential of what they refer to as viral communication, the sprinkling about of sensors like specks of dust that "talk" to one another. The impact on wireless telephony and broadcasting will be immense (unless you prefer to wallow in wires).

Think of community journalists groups as specks in the global village. Distance will no longer be a factor based on advances just in the last decade (check out "The Death of Distance" by Frances Cairncross of The Economist), and high-speed communication will be a given. No more sittin' and a waitin'.

Cairncross writes: "What matters most about a new technology is not how it works, but how people use it, and the changes it brings about in human lives."

Beyond broadening the concept of news coverage, community journalism has the potential to be in the forefront of turning a tide that has swept the U.S. in the past several decades. Prof. Robert D. Putnam's book, "Bowling Alone" (Simon & Shuster, 2000), showed an increasing disconnection between and among individuals that has had impact on just about every social structure from political organizations to churches to, yes, bowling leagues. With blogging, this connectedness would generally be defined as virtual – but an improvement nonetheless; with community journalism face-to-face interchange is more likely.

The mainstream media dabbled in the realm of the consumer-as-creator in the 90's, but seemed to misjudge its potential and abandoned serious research. Much of the grassroots experimentation was being initiated by universities, such as Northwestern, Wisconsin and M.I.T. What follows is some of the seed work that came out of the Media Lab.

FRESHMAN FISHWRAP (Early Nineties)

The Media Lab challenged five freshmen to develop a cutting-edge project, under the tutelage of Walter Bender, then heading the News-in-the-Future consortium of about 30 companies, and doctoral student Pascal Chesnais, later of France Telecom. The students came up with a personalized daily online newspaper called Freshman FishWrap that was used campus-wide and carried news feeds from Associated Press, Reuters, Knight Ridder, Gannett, etc. FishWrap put the news consumer in the driver's seat. Based on survey responses, the system knew when you logged on, who you were, where you were from and what your topical interests were. Readers could organize their news in any way they wished, but most liked their hometown news first, state second, then national and world. FishWrap even had an automated, personalized weather cartoon called Weather Guy. The left panel would have Guy saying, "If you were in San Diego (or whatever the student's home town was), the temperature would be 90 degrees, and it would be sunny . . ." The right panel would say, " . . . but instead you are in Cambridge where it's 19 and will snow today." The site was interactive in a variety of ways, and student users liked to write reviews. One was a review of the ethnic food trucks that gather at mid-day toward the center of campus. Another poplar feature was the community Page One. It became the first item most readers looked at. If you were reading a story that you thought would be of high interest to others in your community, you clicked a button at the top of the story. It created a Top-Stories headline list. The most-clicked story was at the top. For about three years the San Francisco Chronicle's SFgate.com experimented with FishWrap on its site, enabling news junkies to compare the differences in story interests between MIT and Bay readers. Tech, foreign news and rock were big at MIT; Far East news, social issues and music/entertainment at SFgate.

FishWrap was criticized in the media for pandering to the reader. That's a hoot. Translation: The media knows better than the reader in what order the news should be offered up. Apparently it is thought that the crime and grime that almost always opens the local radio and TV news broadcasts is what's best for the public. Or if you are a sports fan, you shouldn't pull out that last section first in your newspaper. Or if you are a senior citizen, you should wait till you get to Page 80 to read the obituary page. Interestingly, fifteen years later, major websites are offering personalization and personalized email feeds.

FOUR CORNERS WEBSITE

Alan Shaw, a doctoral student at the MIT Media Lab, and his wife, Michelle, a Harvard Law School graduate, lived with their young family in a poor neighborhood of about 5000 called Four Corners. It was in the Dorchester section of Boston. Violence was a part of everyday life there, so they started working with the teenagers, teaching them how to fix small appliances for seniors. The goal was to create a dialogue between young and old, because so much misunderstanding had occurred. They were trying to recapture "the good old days" when adults sat out on their front porch steps in the early evening and traded comments with teens strolling past. That doesn't happen anymore in dangerous neighborhoods.

At a summer school, the Shaws taught the teens how to use and repair computers. That led to the development of a Mac-based project called MUSIC (multi-user sessions in community). The teens and the Shaws were the administrators. Since it had audio – even in the early nineties – the users ranged in age from 5 to 85. A system was worked out whereby a person who owned a computer would share it with three or four neighbors (this technique was also successful in another Shaw project in a major Trenton, N.J. development).

When the Four Corners project first started, the Boston Globe decided to participate by feeding a half-dozen electronic versions of stories from that day's Globe into the Four Corners website. The stories ranged from police or City Hall news to recipes to advice columns on child-rearing. A small but early form of media/citizen journalism partnership.

SilverStringer staff surrounds author. Media Lab director Walter Bender on floor.

SILVERSTRINGERS

At an MIT meeting of six or eight faculty and staff in 1996, as described earlier, it was suggested we examine the list of 300 projects going on at the Media Lab by age quartiles. Despite a lot of community activity, the list showed little of it directed specifically toward seniors.

A new senior center had opened 10 miles away in Melrose, and the director was known to be a positive-thinking person, so a Media Lab delegation went to the center, met with some volunteers and soon a community website evolved.

JUNIOR JOURNAL

M.I.T. President Jerome Wiesner, Nicholas Negroponte and a small cadre of researchers had founded the Media Lab in 1978. When Negroponte is mentioned in the press, he's usually referred to as a futurist. An example occurred in 1998.

That was the year the MIT Media Lab hosted something called the Junior Summit, a weeklong meeting of 92 children from around the world who had been selected by 2000 other children, essentially as their representatives, to come up with concrete plans to improve the lot of young people everywhere.

"Set up a newsroom in the classroom off the lower lobby," Negroponte instructed a week before the Summit. And so the desks were shuffled around with some of them strung together to look like a city desk, some books were brought in and some framed photos of news events were hung.

MIT students set up workstations around the edges. The computers were loaded with the "Pluto" publishing software being used by the SilverStringers. No one could figure out why all the furniture was being moved around.

The answer quickly became apparent during the summit's "coffee" break the first morning (the Summit had meetings and field trips scheduled Monday through Friday from 9 a.m. to 9 p.m.). Goodies were served in the lower lobby for about 20 minutes during which time about 30 of the inquisitive young delegates wandered into the adjacent converted classroom.

"What does your software do?" one asked.

"Can I try it? What do you use if for? O, an online newspaper?"

"We want to do that," said another.

"When?" someone asked.

Three or four of them answered in unison: "Today!"

Thus was born the Junior Journal. On that first day they somehow published 21 stories and 17 photos and liked the idea so much that they published every day that week – in between hot-and-heavy meetings. Then they decided they wanted to keep it going as a monthly after they returned home, and they did, starting January 1, 1999.

More detail about the adventures of the SilverStringers and Junior Journalists will unfold in subsequent chapters.

OTHER SPINOFFS

Within a few years of the SilverStringers and the JJ (Junior Journal) startups, new versions spun off, involving adults, teens and even elementary-age children. Three senior sites popped up within 15 miles of Melrose, another in Finland and another in Ireland, where five Stringers were invited to get the ball rolling. In Thailand, a small summer expedition of MIT students and faculty traveled in 1998 to five remote villages where literally overnight, again, the high school-age students got the publishing software working via dish satellite.

Other high school groups discovered the easy-to-use software in Costa Rica, Mexico, India and the U.S. (Gwinnett High School in Georgia). And McGraw-Hill adapted the software as a research-writing complement to its elementary school textbooks, starting throughout Texas, then California and other states soon thereafter. The program was called eJournal.

The most dramatic uses have been in Brazil and Italy. In Curitiba, Brazil, one hundred high school groups published under the auspices of a major media group, Agencia Estado (*www.extraextra.com.br*). In Italy some 7400 middle schools and high schools, according to a count in 2008, became subsections of the Kataweb site produced by La Republicca, a major newspaper. The huge school grouping is called

LaFragola (http://www.lafragola.kataweb.it/fragola/index.jsp), which translated means "strawberry".

When a LaFragola school group comes up with a good story, it gets pulled onto the front page of Kataweb. Suddenly the teens are a part of setting the agenda in their country.

What's happening in Italy is more than a subtle hint as to what the future holds with the advent of citizen journalism.

CHAPTER TWO

Getting Started

> *"You want to be a movie critic?*
> *. . . You are a movie critic."*
>
> **Roger Ebert on** *Cybershake,*
> **WBZ-AM Radio, January 2, 2003**

MOVE OVER, YOGI Berra. Three senior community-journalists-to-be stood around a computer monitor in the Summer of 1996. It was the first time they had laid eyes on Microsoft Windows 95. "Everything starts with start," they were told.

It became a running joke, and yet it sometimes helped to demystify the plunge into the seemingly scary digital world. Starting a community-journalism group shouldn't differ much from organizing a game of poker or forming a discussion club.

Usually there is an instigator who gets the process off the ground, but crowning that person as king or queen could be a mistake. In community settings there's a need for every member to have equal footing. Tortuous decision-making may result, but the benefits outweigh the hand wringing.

Financial costs can be minimal. All that's needed is a place to meet, access to a computer server, publishing software, an internet address and the will. An Internet Service Provider (ISP), for a fee, can register the domain name, which generally would have an .org ending for non-profits. That enables users to reach the site on the internet when they type in *www.whoever.org*. A range of other services can be purchased from web hosting to an email address for the site so the users can give feedback. That feedback can be directed to one person or a dozen. **Recommended: That feedback should go to two persons, one who handles "letters to the editor" and another who acts as a backup**. Web hosting is an added expense. Often servers in a community have space that can accommodate a site free of charge or for a nominal monthly annual fee, but for journalistic reasons some care must be taken in the selection. Use of a governmental site, for instance, could be seen as compromising aggressive coverage; use of a religious institution server could raise questions of favoritism. Some universities are open to use of servers for community groups with no strings attached.

Here's a quick needs-assessment overview:

Publishing:
Minimum of 4-6 participants to start but preferably 10-12
A place to meet regularly in person (or can be via email)
An agreement on the type of content to be published
A schedule for frequency of publication
Access to technical and journalistic expertise if practical
Deadline for story submission to editors

Phase two:
An operations structure and schedule
Recruiting for more members
Orientation for new participants
Stockpile of at least ten stories
Publish

Phase three:
Develop a mission statement and annual goals
-0-

Tools:
Publishing software
A server
An Internet Service Provider or Web Host
Pencil/paper; typewriter; computer.
Access to digital camera, scanner, printer

Exercise:
Write autobiography (100 to 300 words)
Homework: Rewrite autobiography

Starting up is similar from group to group, mostly boiling down to the need to develop confidence that members can perform publishing tasks they had previously thought were only achievable by professionals.

But what took a several weeks of preparation in Melrose and later in Rye was telescoped into a few hours for the Junior Journal:

Here's the actual written at-a-glance the young journalists came up with for content on their very first day, with the understanding that a few stories might take a day or two to get done and be published in later editions:

JUNIOR SUMMIT STORY LIST :
(Need to decide Monday night: Name of publication, sections, what stories will be published TONIGHT, what stories will be finished tomorrow; Who will do stories or photos that have not been assigned yet.)

NEWS
    FirstDay (Josh Matic, Marina Copola, Jose Henrique Bortoluci)
    SuperTopics (Nicole McLaren, etc.)
    TaskForces:
    NationOne (Bruno Gerondi) w/pix by Nusrah Wal, Bruno Gerondi
    The Party (Eduardo Neto) w/pix by Nicole McLaren
    Workshops (???) w/pix by Akiko Doi

INTERVIEWS
    Visiting Press (Hilary McQuaide)
    Norm Chomsky (Mary Fister)
    Chaperones
    Parents (Henrik Hansen)
    Special People
    Justine Cassell interview (Dorothy Okatch)
    Organizers (Dorothy Okatch) w/pix by Dorothy)

FEATURES
    Food Critique (Manal Ahmad) w/pix by Dorothy Okatch
    Cultures at Summit (Karabo Morule)
    MUDs (Eduardo Neto)
    Satirical Column (Makonnen Blake)
    Children's Views of News

TECHNOLOGY
Pagers (Jacqueline Wright)
Computing skills (Jeff Gu and Zhao Yue) w/pix by Jeff

PHOTOGRAPHY
Hotel (Henrik Hansen and Don Sying)
Delegates layout (Nusrah Wal, Aikiko Doi, Agna)
Media Lab
Essay (Mary Fister)
Fashion Show (Nicole McLaren, Henrik Hansen, Jose Saavedra, Nusrah Wali)

ART
Art Gallery
Cartoon Page

GAMES
Quiz Page (Nusrah Wal)
Fun Page
Game applets

AUDIO/VIDEO
Real Audio Translations
Real Video of Conferences

Besides discovering publishing software during their soft-drink break that first day, the soon-to-be Junior Journalists also got a chance to meet a few MIT students who had volunteered to help them. The "rock star" was shy sophomore Dennis Quan, who the year before at age 16 had written most of the publishing software that essentially would be used by the Media Lab network for the next decade. He was not much older than most of them.

The summiteers decided they needed an afternoon meeting. With the help of Prof. Brian Smith, who relates well to young people, and graduate student/grandmother Ingeborg Endter, who had been working with the SilverStringers, they were given a quickie seminar on the realities of publishing that afternoon. Several had to have interpreters to understand what was being said. A 10-year-old blonde with a red beret fell asleep at her workstation (She later became an editor). It wasn't long before two more her age, then another, conked out. Otherwise it was raucous. They were pumped up, interrupted frequently with lots of good questions but generally wanted more action and fewer words. It was then about 4 o'clock.

Out of the Minds of Babes

Karabo Morule of South Africa
(Dona Tversky photo)

In the time needed to take a deep breath they decided they didn't want an editor-in-chief. It would be a group effort. They chose Karabo Morule, 16, of South Africa as the editor-for-the-day. It turned out to be a brilliant choice, particularly when you considered they all had only met in person a few hours earlier. She wrote several stories, contributed seven photos – including some notable ones from a dinner/tour at the Science Museum – and generally was cool under fire. A 10-year-old volunteered to write the lead story (ages were supposed to range from 10 to 16 at the summit, but one "reporter" admitted he was 9).

The main story was a roundup of the day's events. Two other attendees jumped in to help the 10-year-old write it. Group writing is a cumbersome process that even seasoned professionals stumble through. But the untested trio pulled it off. Other stories were about the various groups the 92 children were broken up into during a day of endless, exhausting debate on poverty, environment, child labor, child soldiers, new technology, etc.

They also assigned interviews of the visiting press, of Prof. Norm Chomsky, the chaperones, some parents, Prof. Justine Cassell of the Media Lab, the multi-lingual director of the summit, and other organizers.

The best story of the first day was a review on the food. They didn't like it. The best story of the week was about a nightly party that went on at the hotel. They liked it.

A pause at party in Room 818.

On the final day of the Summit at MIT's Kresge Auditorium before a jam-packed crowd, many of whom represented private companies, the participants presented concrete plans that came out of their weeklong discussions for group activities that would carry forward. One plan was to continue the "Junior Journal".

Nicholas Negroponte promised access to a server for five years and other Media Lab help. Business Week said it would help, and so too did Reuters. The Junior Journalists were on their way.

The Marching Orders

Exhilarated yet exhausted as they packed to leave, they asked me to put down on paper what they had agreed to and what the overall plan should be. Meanwhile, they dragged themselves back to China and South Africa and Pakistan and California and Morocco and India and Brazil and Argentina and elsewhere to catch up on their sleep and their school work. Their marching orders they asked me to compile, based on their own decision making, went out to them by email a few weeks after the Summit and read as follows:

"OK! Here we go. Ten of you have signed up to be Editors so far.

"The ten are: Bruno Gerondi, Hilary McQuaide, Nusrah Wali, Spyros Gelepis, Mary Fister (maryf), Manal M. Ahmad, Deepika Rosanne Pereira, Yiting Li, Jeff Gu and Shehzad Shahid Khan. Karabo Morule also wishes to be an Editor but will only be able to work in a limited capacity for a while, because she was just named to the prestigious and demanding position of Head Girl for 1999 at her school. Also, I have not heard from a couple of others who I expect will want to work with the editing team

"Now what?

"First, you should decide on some assignments as quickly as possible. The deadline for stories and photos to be sent to the Editors Basket is December 20. You plan to publish on January 1, 1999. That will give you Editors 10 days to edit the stories, send them back for revision if necessary, and do the final editing by Dec. 31.

"How will we do this? Do you want me to pick one of you to be the assigning editor for ALL stories this month given the short time left? (I'll write your names on pieces of paper, crumble them, throw them in the air and pick one). The January-Edition Editor could then give at least one assignment to each of you and ask you to: contact one delegate to write the story, send it to the Editors Basket, and then you do the editing when it arrives.

"Second, several delegates at the summit told me they want to write. Recently I heard from Nicole McLaren, Sonali Unkule, and Jacqueline Wright to say they are interested . . .

"In the questionnaire I sent out, everyone said "yes" to every question except #4 and #5. Some thought it would be good to pick one person to design the front; others thought it best to have several try and pick the best one. Bruno has already designed a front, and Ingeborg has put it in the Public Storage section of the Junior Journal. If your design is in HTML or you make a picture of it, you can upload it into the Public Storage section for all to see. During the week of Dec. 21, I will send out a note, asking you as the Editors to vote on your favorites. Somewhere on the front page of the Junior Journal should be a place to tell the name of the group and the general purpose of the website. What should you say is the general purpose? . . .

"More questions I will need answers to from you:

a. Do you want me to randomly pick one of you to be January-edition Editor?

b. Would it be a good idea to have two editors edit each story. Editor One would edit the story as well as possible, then pass it on to Editor Two for a double check. Finally, the January Editor would hit the Publish button on the last day of the month.

c. Would you like to be considered as February-edition or March-edition Editor?

d. If there are editing questions, do you want me to be your sounding board by email for a while?

e. Do you agree that any delegate can be a reporter?

f. Do you agree that any of the other 2000 participants who were not delegates can be a reporter if they contact the Administrative Editor to get a name and password into the Journal?

g. Who wants to be Administrative Editor for six months, working by email with Ingeborg Endter of MIT?

h.   Do you prefer to have (A) one issue or topic each month that gets special attention or (B) a mix: some stories emphasizing one topic and others on a variety of topics? Pick A or B.

i.   Who will respond to Feedback from readers when it's necessary to do so?

j.   Should you have one editor in charge of each section or is that necessary?

k.   Can someone from each Action Plan be responsible for updating material in their subsections when necessary (whatever they do should go through an editor before being published, so they should send material to the Editors Basket)?

l.   Is it acceptable to have the January issue appear in English if we are unable to get the translation system working in time? (I would urge reporters to write in their native language and for the time being let us at MIT figure out how to translate the stories when we see them in the Editors Basket)?

Other issues to be thinking about, and we'll discuss later:

a.   How do you get a good geographic mix of stories?

b.   How do you get good photos or art to go with the stories?

c.   Do you want guest-of-the-month articles from adults (one suggestion was to ask Bill Gates, Nicholas Negroponte, Nelson Mandela and other well-known persons to write for the Journal). Cheers, jack driscoll"

And away they went, publishing their first edition after the Summit in January of 1999 and never stopping until 2005.

A Small-Town Experiment

Shortly after the Junior Journal went into limbo after seven mind-boggling years, Rye Reflections came on the scene.

Rye, N.H., was a good test for a community-journalism site because of the town's small size (12.6 square miles), its population (about 5200) and its history as having been the site of the first New Hampshire settlement in 1623. It is located about 55 miles north of Boston, just south of Portsmouth on the N.H. seacoast. Rye Reflections started off without a hitch.

Scratch deeply enough, and you'll find that every hamlet has its own soul, its own specialness, its own stories to be told. "I think people have a natural-born tendency to tell stories. There's poetry in each and every one of us," said Studs Terkel, the author-radio interviewer who often described himself as a "guerrilla journalist with a tape recorder."[1]

A stone's throw from one of the beaches in Rye is the Cable House, a nondescript gabled structure of the type that is common along the coast of New England. This one, however, made an indelible mark on the history of communications.

At this location in 1874 a transcontinental cable was completed, connecting Britain, Newfoundland, Nova Scotia and the United States with 3,104 miles of what was called "duplex cable". The submerged cable enabled two-way simultaneous messaging.[2] It was the ultimate in one-to-one communication. (You could say we now have the penultimate: multipoint to multipoint interactivity). The cable station operated for 47 years, initially manned by 16 telegraphers from England, Scotland, Wales and Ireland. Commercial aspirations spurred this painstaking project, but part of the impetus also was derived from the inner desire we all have to communicate as rapidly as possible with others near and far. We either have information to convey or we have a need for information someone else possesses.

The means of expression have gone from the simple to the sublime: drawings on clay tablet, papyrus, cuneiform, alphabets, printing presses, Morse code, wire and wireless transmission; radio, still photography, cinema, video, the computer and the internet.

With or without wires, we now have nearly instant access to words, sounds and images, thanks to the digital explosion whose full impact may not be realized for decades. Even now we don't know fully how this new plateau of information flow will impact our lives and our world.

And so in Rye in late March, 2005, a small group of citizens gathered to form a website. They started with Start.

A room was reserved for a weekly meeting of interested citizens at the Rye Public Library. The town's three library trustees and its director gave their blessings to the request for space, knowing that the institution of "library" is being redefined by the digital age everywhere. The book depository is transforming into a social center.

STEP ONE: A Space to Meet
STEP TWO: Get Out the Word
STEP THREE: Meet and Just Let It Happen.

The first meeting was planned for mid-March. Meetings thereafter would be weekly, it was announced.

Meetings held without fail once a week create consistency and are a must for monthly publications. If they're held every other week and a participant misses – as is inevitable from time to time – it means the member is out of contact for at least a month, running the risk of that person feeling out of touch and drifting off.

Step No. 2 simply involved posting about 20 sheets of 8 ½ x 11 at local coffee shops, at Town Hall and the Library, at the Post Office and – for sure! – at the Recycling Center. Pamphleteering is pretty competitive everywhere.

A note also was put on the town website and in the town newsletter, along with one-paragraph items carried by three newspapers, their websites and in the calendar of a community radio station in neighboring Portsmouth. Additionally letters of notification went to the chairpersons of an art study group, the garden club and the poetry-writing group.

Despite the advance publicity the first community-journalism meeting had only four participants.

Not a problem. A buzz had been created. At the second meeting there were six, but it was Good Friday. Religious day or not, Fridays, it was learned, are not good for meetings. For many it's getaway day. The meetings were switched to Thursday.

Here's what a one-page posted notice looked like:

COME JOIN US!
Online writing group is organizing in Rye.
Meetings on Thursdays, 2 p.m., Rye Library
No experience needed to write, edit, take photographs, do artwork. (Could use a computer expert or two)

A total of seven showed up for the first Thursday meeting. It took ten weeks of tutorials and preparation to get ready for publication of the first edition, and by that time word-of-mouth had swelled the number of attendees to about 15. Getting hung up on the numbers can be counter-productive. Quality of content is more important than quantity of participants. Folks will come and go, but slowly a foundation of regulars will take hold.

Once the site is up and running it should sell itself. But as the weeks go on, welcoming signals need to ripple out so that it doesn't seem to be another clique. Occasional recruiting drives not only add new voices but also people with new experiences and new perspectives that are uplifting.

The essence of group community journalism is inclusion. The group and the product of its efforts are the richer for it. Sometimes it takes hard work, patience and especially acceptance.

Stacy Horn, who founded an online community called Echo way back in 1989, discusses the issue of tolerance at length in her book "Cyberville."[3] "For a community to work," she wrote, "you have to accept imperfection . . . we are all assholes from time to time."

STEP FOUR: Initial meetings.
STEP FIVE: Balancing journalism and technology.
STEP SIX: The First Edition.

The first meeting emphasized getting comfortable – with one another and with the concept of community publishing.

Someone has to be the facilitator, introducing himself or herself and emphasizing the pivotal themes for community journalism: (1) The value of sharing your wisdom with the community; (2) the personal benefit that derives from social networking within the group.

One ice-breaker involves having attendees introduce themselves by telling one thing about themselves and explaining why they decided to come. The introductory exercise takes a bit of time and is a standard community-building activity that pays short and long-run dividends. Laughter is the best facilitator. Apprehension is the biggest obstacle, even among those who by nature are confident with themselves. They're breaking new ground, and it takes a little coaxing of their self-esteem.

Garrison Keillor probably came up with the best advice for those just starting out: "Be bold, thrust forward, and have the courage to fail. After all it's only writing. Nobody is going to die for your mistakes, or even lose their teeth."[4]

Campfire Analogy

Starting a website may seem like rocket science for newcomers, but it really is an extension of most people's inclination to tell stories, a practice that dates back centuries. A couple of years before Rye Reflections started, performance-artist Laurie Anderson appeared at the Metro Theater in Portsmouth, N.H., a city adjacent to Rye. She said her notion of technology is that it is "the campfire around which we are all now telling our stories."

In the campfire model, storytelling begins where you live. The good stories tend to spread, making their way to other campfires and then beyond.

You can only cover so much in one meeting. Clearly the first meeting is hardly the time to pound out a mission statement. Writing a mission statement can be done later – like, much later; maybe months later. That first meeting, however, is a good time to differentiate between blogs and group journalism, which has the practical value of members feeding off each other to flesh out and enhance their own ideas for content. Brainstorming widens the channels of creativity. It provides added dimension and variety.

Operating in a community setting as part of a flat structure is a sticky wicket for adults, less so for teens. Those who have worked most of their lives have been accustomed to a top-down form of management. In other volunteer activities they have been accustomed to up-or-down voting on issues. The majority rules.

The community model calls for arriving at decisions by consensus. It's time consuming, it's messy, it can be antagonistic at times, but it's better than having a participant simmering in a corner for weeks after voting against an issue or procedure. And some groups have collapsed when the leader has had to leave for one reason or another. Succession-planning is not a common practice in volunteer organizations the way it is in business. As a practical matter, consensus means a question is thrashed out until everyone has had a full say and the group decides to move forward in a certain direction.

Community Process

As an example, the Rye group took portions of three meetings to decide on the name of its publication, "Rye Reflections". Thirty-one suggestions were listed on a whiteboard. A vote would have quickly decided the issue by the numbers, but it was clear that some hated certain contenders and some were madly in love with others, a formula for festering unhappiness if they took a vote.

It took two meetings of discussion to narrow the list to six. After realizing the decision would be forever (probably), the third week of discussion went in circles. Finally an organized woman stood and said she would list the six most-favored names on the whiteboard. She would then poll everyone, one by one, and ask each to state which one name he or she liked best and which he or she liked least. Her husband was the first to speak. "I don't think I like "Rye Reflections'," he said. Quickly she responded, "O yes you do!" Laughter erupted, he relented, a more relaxed atmosphere took hold and a consensus was arrived at in about 10 minutes.

MELROSE MIRROR – In the initial get-together the Media Lab offered a collaboration on a project of their choosing, and it was the Stringers who came up with the concept of a newspaper-in-a computer along with one person's ringing exclamation: "We want to be on the cutting edge". Here are excerpts of the notes from the second meeting, held in 1996 at the city's senior center, which is a converted carriage house.

THURSDAY, JUNE 13 – Bender, Glorianna Davenport, Napolitano and Driscoll met with 10 volunteers and outlined the program. About half were interested in writing, the others were interested in playing supportive roles. Two indicated an interest in writing poetry. Discussion included whether a newsletter or newspaper should be attempted, since they were unfamiliar with the web concept. A healthy debate ensued as to whether stories outside the city of Melrose should be written, and it was generally concluded that there should be no boundaries but that the subject matter for the most part should be of interest to Melrose citizens (an example was reviews on Summer theater performances in a nearby city). Bender asked each person who was interested to produce a story, poem, drawings or photographs a week ahead of the next meeting so that he could show them what their work actually looked like on the internet.

(The MIT Media Lab players were Walter Bender, director of the News-in-the-Future consortium; Prof. Glorianna Davenport, a video documentarian who ran the lab's Interactive Cinema group; Felice Napolitano, Bender's efficient administrative assistant who luckily lived around the corner at that time. Not mentioned was Jack

Beckley, senior center director who had pledged a phone line, a room to meet weekly and other supplies with the understanding that MIT would supply used computer equipment, a scanner and printer).

High tech? Typed stories – and a couple in longhand – plus some photo prints were stuffed in envelopes and left at the senior-center front desk to be picked up by "Felice the Courier" every few days. She and others of us would then either type or scan the material into the system. During one prescient visit Felice took a photo of the carriage house. The SilverStringers liked it so much they made it part of their masthead.

Bender's challenge to produce some content and talk about it later was a little like teaching someone to swim by having them jump into the water. It was a resounding success.

When we returned two weeks later, we brought a ringer, doctoral candidate Pascal Chesnais. He and Bender had designed a website and posted the content: five poems (4 by one person) and a clever story about an upcoming trip in an Airstream travel trailer across the country ("The Little House on Wheels"). Another story on the 150th anniversary of a local order of nuns was written but didn't make its way to MIT in time for this demo.

The group had now grown to 15. After one look at the demo, they were hooked. Questions spilled out: How do you get a story into the system? Where can we find a computer linked to the internet? (Answer: Melrose Library and Senior Center itself, since we were leaving the laptop hooked up in a meeting room that had been designated for the project). Could a glossary of terms be distributed, especially having to do with computer operations? Is there any way to make the type size bigger? How does Microsoft Word work? What about copyright issues? Could instructions be given on how stringers get and write stories?

We had our marching orders. Our work was cut out for us. But the fun had also just begun.

The Palace Coup

Rather than setting a startup date, we were publishing stories as they arrived for several weeks. Instruction was desperately needed in journalistic and technical matters. What's tricky with new groups is how to reach a balance. Half the meeting on content and half on computing? Devote alternating weeks to each?

None of the SilverStringers had ever used Microsoft Word, so we decided they needed to grasp the basics at least, although it appeared one or two had done some word processing in their jobs. Bear in mind, this was 1996. After instructions, some were frightened to even touch the mouse, but before long they were all trying it and clearly were excited. A couple seemed to catch on quickly. "Look at this," said one woman. "I clicked 'Start' and got a list of all these words: 'Programs', 'Documents', 'Find', 'Run' – O dear, I think I'll run!"

As receptive as they were to guidance, they also were determined to steer their own ship. On October 9, only a few months into the project, a bloodless coup occurred. The SilverStringers announced to the MIT delegation that henceforth the Stringers would run the meetings, rotating the chairperson duties every two weeks. They decided to call that person "Coordinator" which, they said, "means an appointed person who will keep participants on focus." They handed out a list and telephone numbers for 14 persons who would be coordinators. Chairpersons would serve in alphabetical order. The group was in charge of its own destiny and never looked back.

REVERE SATTERLIGHTS – When community-journalism groups hook up, good things happen. Less than a year after the SilverStringers started their website, they connected with two women who were part of a program called the Modem Mavens. The women lived in the Satter House, a seniors' complex overlooking the ocean in Revere, Mass., just up the coast from Boston and a few miles from Melrose. It included a neat little computer room where some of the 300 residents were being taught the basics by staff and these two Mavens, who also lived there. On March 19, 1997, Millie Vogel and Ruth Brodsky were invited to a SilverStringers' meeting, and it was love at first sight on both sides. Soon a delegation from Melrose spent an afternoon with a half dozen residents at the Satter House. Three months later, with technical help from the MIT Media Lab, the Revere Satterlights community-journalism site was born. It's a smaller-scale effort, because participation is limited to residents, but the Satterlight site has its own pleasing personality, reflecting the influence of living near the sea and of its members being of Jewish extraction. Several of their pre-immigration stories have been gripping.

Peer-to-peer mentoring has become a hallmark of the SilverStringers who also have given volunteer assistance to groups in Danvers and Brighton, Mass., Ennis, Ireland, and Rye, N.H.

THAILAND – In the summer of 1998 delegations from MIT headed for Thailand to explore the use of technology for schooling in remote villages, one that had a population of only 600. The trip was said to grow out of a discussion between Nicholas Negroponte and the king of Thailand, who wanted to experiment with ways to upgrade the education system. The group packed a disk with Media Lab software, now called Pluto (had been Goofy; later version was Huey, Dewey & Louie), because it's easy to learn. Youngsters spent the mornings working in the fields, then went to school in the afternoon at a community building. The MIT group set up satellite dishes in at least two of the villages, and, somehow, the Thai children published the very first day. Here's the report posted on the web by the mostly-student MIT delegation in both English and Thai languages:

On-line Community Magazine Workshop
Mae Fah Luang (Thailand)
July 8-17, 1998

> *This workshop was conducted in a rural village in northern Thailand. As part of the Lighthouse project, a satellite with Internet connection was installed. There were 45 participants. Some of them were children from nearby hill tribes, others were rural teachers and others were delegates from different pilot sites involved in the Lighthouse project.*
>
> *The goal of the workshop was to help people create an on-line community magazine within the constructionist approach to education. This means that the process of journalistic authorship, revision and critique was as important as the final product. Another key element of this workshop was to contribute to people's technological fluency, in this case, using the Internet, HTML and Pluto, a software specially designed at the Media Lab's News in the Future Consortium to support this type of electronic publishing.*
>
> *The workshop was conducted at Mae Fah Luang by doctoral students Mike Best and Marina Umaschi Bers and Media Lab's alum Josh Bers. Pipe Tuchinda, a Thai MIT undergraduate student, also helped with the workshop. In Boston, on the MIT front, Ingeborg Endter and Dennis Quan constantly helped with Pluto's support and bug fixes.*
>
> *You can visit the Mae Fah Luang on-line community magazine (most of it is in Thai so you need to install the Thai font to be able to read it. But there is a significant amount of work in English and you can always look at the pictures).*

After the delegation left, the program continued at several locations, but word seeped back regarding a glitch at one village. It seems the parents decided the children were having too much fun at school. Something had to be amiss, they thought. So, as a group, they ordered their children to stop using the computers. The children became so unhappy the parents decided to examine the situation more deeply and soon figured out what this computing attraction was all about. Indeed, they realized they could sell their homemade jewelry to nearby villages via the internet, and suddenly it all made sense. We assume everyone lived happily ever after, or something like that.

BRAZIL – In the U.S., newspapers have been active in a widely-acclaimed program called Newspaper-in-the-Classroom. Teachers are trained how to use the daily newspaper as a teaching tool in a variety of subjects. Math comes alive in baseball boxscores. Why shouldn't the publishers forge partnerships with schools to facilitate student online publications? Grupo Estado, a major media company in Sao Paulo, Brazil, quickly picked up on the idea in 1999 when Agencia Estado website director Rodrigo Mesquita invited Walter Bender, Prof. Brian Smith, researcher David Cavallo and me to Sao Paulo to meet with 125 high school teachers to explain how the alliance would work. A short while later, under the supervision of the Secretary of Education, 11 schools in the district of Curitiba completed a pilot project and shortly thereafter 100 schools were publishing their versions of what they called "ExtraExtra". The Education Director, Prof. Denise Maria Chella Machado, referred to the program as "our pride" in a press release. The students tended to use more video than the highly successful La Fragola school sites referred to in Chapter One.

GEORGIA – Meanwhile, a different spin on the same concept was being fashioned by Bell South with the high school in South Gwinnett, near Atlanta. Bell South provided the server and other assistance, MIT the software. First called teenstringers. com and later Cometsonline.com, it fed off an advanced technology program at the school, buoyed by an enthusiastic adviser and lots of support from the top at the school. Maybe too much. Is there a subtle stifling factor for teenagers who have to operate under a school system, with all its understandable strictures, as opposed to the total-independence model exhibited by the Junior Journal in which the burden of responsibility totally rests with the teens?

Many more questions will be raised and answered; much more will be learned about all the manifestations of community journalism. But getting started is the least of the problems.

CHAPTER THREE

The Basic Tools

*"Communities become demanding
when they're engaged. They have
a heightened sense of commitment."*

**Walter Bender, MIT Media Laboratory
In Editor & Publisher, July 1997**

T HE UNITED PRESS bureau in
Boston had elaborate systems for
internal communication 50 years ago. A key "technology" was the spike. When
a correspondent called in a story, the reporter who took the information over the
phone would write a payment figure (usually $1) on a small piece of paper with the
correspondent's name and a date and slam the note down on a spike. At the end of
the day all the little chunks of paper would be lifted off the spike and collated.

Paper flew in a variety of directions in that operation. Stories were written on
what were called "books". The news clerk was the bookmaker. Periodically he would
sit at his desk with a stack of tissue-thin yellow sheets on one side and carbon paper
on the other. As fast as his hands could move, the clerk would merge the two. Each
book was made up of six sheets and five carbons, stapled together. Up to 500 books
were made a day, a sure recipe for a sore neck.

Reporters used typewriters in those days, so each writer had a supply of books.
The original sheet went to the TTS operator (that's teletype setter) who punched the
story onto a tape, ready for transmission. The reporter kept a copy; another went to

the radio desk; another to the so-called Pony Express (UP sent packages of certain stories to some afternoon newspapers by train); another went to the night crew, and the sixth had to be filed.

The system worked flawlessly, because there was a basket designated for each copy to be placed in; sort of a form of normal office workflow: in basket, out basket, mail basket, interoffice basket, etc.

Stan Berens, who later became Bureau Chief, was known as one of the fastest, best wire-service writers in the business. He always wrote with a cigarette dangling from his mouth. Even with glasses and his head always slightly tilted back, he had to keep his eyes half shut to prevent the smoke from searing them. He had a congenital hip problem, so he sat with his long, spindly legs crossed to the side of his typewriter platform and typed almost sidesaddle. Every story was started the same way. He'd type a few words, maybe even a paragraph, then – R-I-P! – he'd tear the "book" out of the typewriter and throw it in the wastebasket. After a half-dozen false starts, he'd get up a head of steam like a truck plunging downhill and write the story from top to bottom.

Virtual Baskets

Years later the backend of the Media Lab's publishing software was patterned after that simple process. After logging on, a user sees a variety of baskets, depending upon how the group sets thing up. The primary basket is called Your Basket. That's where the user keeps stories and photos that are being prepared for publication. Once the story is ready, it can easily be sent to the Editors Basket. Once edited, the story is sent to the Publishing Basket where it sits awaiting publication day.

Those who aren't particularly computer literate seem to adjust easily to the basket system after the comparison with office baskets is made. And they quickly learn how to transfer material from one basket to another.

Any number of baskets may be created, depending on the group's needs. A writer might only have access to four baskets, while an editor can get into six or seven and an administrator may have access to as many as ten. For instance:

INTRODUCTION BASKET – Explains how the software works and provides a short tour. Access by all.

YOUR BASKET – A place to write stories and store them until they are completed. Also a basket to store photos or other text/media files. Only the author and administrator have access to this basket.

EDITORS BASKET – Where stories are sent for editing. Editor-access only.

PUBLISHING BASKET – Where fully edited stories are sent to await publication. Limited access.

PHOTO-CANDIDATE BASKET – Only for photos to be considered for use in the upcoming issue. Access by all.

PROTECTED BASKET – Where stories are sent for safekeeping – and access if necessary – after publication. Limited access.
EDIT-SECTIONS BASKETS – Where section and article templates reside, along with all articles and media organized by sections. Limited access.
PUBLIC-STORAGE BASKET – For non-publication material, such as minutes of meetings, policies, special instructions. Access by all.
ARCHIVE BASKET – A place where published template, section, article and media material is kept. Limited access.
DISCUSSION BASKET – Where issues can be discussed by group members in between meetings. Open access.
ADMINISTRATION BASKET – Where site administrator manages user information, logs, templates and the like. Limited access.

For groups the backend of software is where the work is done. Some of that work entails collaboration; some work might be considered housekeeping and requires a modicum of technical skill.

Despite improved, simplified software, every group needs at least one – preferably two or three – persons with technical expertise at the start and on a continuing basis. Some in the group will learn a lot of the technical ropes because of need or curiosity or just because it's fun, while others may never have the inclination. That's what makes community: People with varying interests who accept each other as they are.

Before walking through a couple of my hands-on experiences, let me in layman's terms (1) describe some of the hardware needs; (2) software needs; (3) other resources; (4) some of the decisions that need to be made whether technical, non-technical or a bit of both. Regarding Point Four, the process of the Junior Journal is captured in some detail, because communication was all by email after the Junior Summit, so all-in-writing preparation provides a rare glimpse into most of the issues a group will grapple with orally. (Imagine how ignorant we would be without what we learn from children.)

Essential Hardware Needs

Conceivably a group could function at a meeting place without a computer. Somewhere, however, there has to be a server, loaded with the appropriate software, that can be connected to by members and readers through a URL (uniform resource locator), better known as an address, such as *www.yourgroupname.org*.

The audience would get to your website through that address; members would have an assigned name and password to get into the back end of the site where created material is stored, edited and prepared for publication.

A basic server generally suffices, and it doesn't matter where it's located. More than 300 Junior Journal participants lived in 91 countries around the world and operated for several years through a server in Cambridge, Mass., USA. Most of the computing work – editing, writing, photo/art handling – can be done from home or wherever there's a computer connected to the internet. Even the publishing of an edition can be done by one person at home if need be, but it's more fun to have a few people working together on that final, fulfilling step.

For years the SilverStringers held their meetings in a senior-center conference room without a computer. Their equipment was down the hall in another room. After a few years they discovered that the optimal setup was to have one computer in the meeting room connected to the internet on one end and to a projector on the other. They use a blank wall for show & tell. If a published story or photo is being discussed, it is flashed onto the wall. If they need to walk a member through some how-to steps, it can be done right then and there in a blown-up form rather than on a computer monitor screen. They also can call up other websites that might come up in discussions. For ten years they worked with a slow telephone connection to the internet, but the lack of speed didn't deter them. The Rye group, on the other hand, had the advantage of the Public Library's fast wireless connection with a laptop tied to a projector right from the start.

In the years ahead the accelerating speed of internet connections and more user-friendly software will make group journalism even easier and more enjoyable.

It's a luxury for a group to have access to a computer room in a building (community center, YMCA/YWCA, school, church, senior center, library, retirement facility, etc.). Two or three computers with some peripherals can constitute a computer room. It is also a venue for the less computer-literate to learn from one another. On one occasion three Lotus researchers who were working on design issues attended a SilverStringers meeting. "We're interested in developing parameters for how tasks are performed by older persons," said a Lotus visitor.

"We don't know how we do it," a SilverStringer retorted.

"Or we don't remember," said another.

They then provided serious responses, having to do with the design of the keyboard ("could the letters be bigger?"), the need for ways to help them remember how to perform certain tasks they do infrequently, the value of a good "help" system, understandable terminology, one-on-one instruction especially by the "right person". In regard to the last point, they said that compatibility is important for useful instruction. As is often the case, the Stringers had wise advice, even when being humorous. Russ Priestley, who among other things was a test pilot during World War II, said, "I think the best way is for the instructor to stand up and the student to sit down." When laughter subsided, he added in all seriousness: "The student should be at the controls; get the feel."

A printer and scanner near or in the meeting place are useful. A digital camera that can be borrowed like a book can be convenient for a group to possess, although more and more individuals have their own cameras. For the spontaneous shot, carrying your own digital camera can be a plus. Camcorders are also starting to be used more and more by community journalists who have learned that short clips work best on a website. Ability to edit video is getting easier and easier, even for the novice. Lots of attention – even from former Vice President Al Gore – has been devoted to facilitating video publishing by average citizens in the last few years. Among the pioneers was *www.ourmedia.org*, a non-profit.

Public/Private Sides of Software

Off-the-shelf software of late has tended to become easier and easier to use by the uninitiated and less and less expensive. If everyone in the group threw a few dollars into a hat, it probably would cover the cost for starting up and maintaining a site. Registering a site name is a one-time cost, again not exorbitant. Rye registered as a non-profit with a web-hosting service for five years at a cost of $60 in 2005.

The writer-editor dynamic is where commonsenseware best comes into play. A smooth flow of communication should exist between editors and writers, whether they are working for a metropolitan newspaper or a community website. Communication generally is unnecessary for non-substantive word or sentence changes, smoothing out, tightening up, cutting down and the like, but any rewriting or inserting of material or alteration should be done in consultation with the writer. A whole book could be done on this subject, including the various tricks editors and writers use to avoid talking to one another, but suffice it to say that in community journalism the tilt should be toward leaving stories the way they are written rather than imposing Harper's Magazine standards. Encouraging discussion is the best way to avoid bad feelings.

Dozens of commercial software packages have evolved over the last decade. Indeed, some of the software developed for bloggers is adaptable for groups. In blogging you have single-person production; in groups you have a collaboration involving a workflow system with editorial dialogue built in. In either case pre-editing of writing, pictures, audio and video is usually required on your personal computer before content is put into the collaborative mix. For instance, with Adobe Photoshop or more simple-to-use software you can crop, size and sharpen photos before uploading them into your group file system.

Having group forms or templates for such items as poetry or letters to the editor is useful so that they will all have the same style when published, thus giving the website a consistent look. When Junior Journal editors tried to use the same headline style for poetry that they had for stories, they soon found themselves in trouble. The story-headline style allowed so many words that the editors often found themselves saying more than the poem was trying to say. After a few months they adopted a style for a one-line title, usually containing nouns and adjectives, as compared with headlines that work best with verbs.

Sheer Enthusiasm

Sure, the Junior Journalists cranked out five editions in the week they were at MIT, but it was mostly a product of passion and adrenaline. They cared deeply about the issues they were grappling with. And, for a change, they were speaking with their own voices without a parental or adult filter. They weren't going to let any operational details get in their way. Perhaps Stanford Business School should develop a case study around what they pulled off.

After gaining approval to continue the publication they started during the Junior Summit, the young journalists left for home, going off in every conceivable direction. In the circular driveway of their hotel that Saturday night bedlam reigned as they ran from one to another, hugging, crying, screaming and then, one by one, collapsing into taxis to head for the airport and their trips to Casablanca and Shanghai and Delhi and Athens and Johannesburg and Sao Paulo and Nairobi and Paris and Lahore and Buenos Aires and San Francisco . . .

Once they had returned to their neighborhoods and school challenges would they forget the Junior Journal? A couple of days went by. The email circuits were starkly silent. Jet lag? And then the following (excerpted) arrived from a US participant:

Hi you guys!

Well. I arrived home safely and was depressed at the thought of going to school the next day and not riding the bus with you all to the Media Lab, and those were the first memories that hit me Blair doing some crazy dance down the aisle of the bus; Eduardo and Leon staring at me to make me laugh; jokes with Nicole about the "couple" sitting in the seats in front of us; our terribly funny trolley car driver with her joke attempts; pictures of Sasha asleep against Yiting's shoulder; everyone passing posters around for others to sign on the bus home from Saturday's presentation; busy reading and writing on our incredibly cool pagers at all hours of the day, especially all bus rides.

Well, to say the least, I was disappointed to be home. It would be so much more fun to still be at MIT with all of the great people I had the pleasure to meet over the past week! Unfortunately though I am home, and I'm so happy that I have such wonderful memories to last me a lifetime.

I'll always remember the parties in room 818, the blackhole; ordering pizza and then convincing the counselors to stay until it was delivered; looking across the breakfast table at all the groggy eyes from staying out so late at night; loading the bus with our color groups every morning (tradition with Nicole, always walking out of the hotel together so we'd be better

prepared to face the cold). I'll cherish the memories of picture time, how we'd start out with one camera and end up having to pose for 50 cameras to record the picture; the busy hours brainstorming in the cube or talking to media; the food; AND ESPECIALLY ALL THE GREAT FRIENDS I MADE!!! ...
Much Love,
Hilary McQuaide
WAITING TO HEAR FROM EVERYONE!!!

Hilary (one L) of Junior Journal with then-presidential candidate Hillary (two L's) Clinton.

The lid was off. Email began to fly, especially among the 32 who signed up for the Junior Journal. Over the next several years JJ members were exchanging 20 to 40 messages a day on the weekdays, fewer on the weekends. The tone, while often laced with humor, reflected their determination to have their voices heard, as they often would say. That was their cause. They wanted to change the world.

Story ideas, operational issues, policy questions ... All had to be sorted out by email. The technology was the facilitator. There were only five weeks between the end of the Summit and their first monthly publication. Critical major decisions already had been set in cement: the Junior Journal name, publication monthly, a board of editors with a rotating editor in charge of each edition, a January 1, 1999 starting date. At the editors' request I sent out a basic questionnaire, asking that they reaffirm that they wished to participate and raising such questions as:

- Could you as a group design a general look for the front of the website?
- What sections do you want? I listed some, such as News, Features, Entertainment and Opinion along with sections for their ongoing task forces such as Kids Bank, Hope Olympics, Nurturing Awareness, Education.
- Should there be an Administrative Editor to handle setting up new reporters with passwords and baskets and ironing out technical details?
- Can you pull this off in time for a fresh publication by January 1, despite the interruptions of Ramadan, Hanukkah and Christmas.

Their answers came back quickly. They used consensus rather than voting to decide on a variety of questions. They decided to have a contest among participants to design a logo. Bruno Gerondi of Argentina came up with the winner:

They decided the editor-of-the-month could choose the look of the page. They decided the sections would be Editorial, News, Features, Opinion, Poetry, People, Culture, Photo Gallery and Entertainment and that all of the task forces could submit stories to a section called "Action Projects". Choosing sections not only is an important first step toward organizing a website but also crucial, because you don't want to keep changing names of sections. In the beginning it's best to pick as few sections as possible. Adding later is better than subtracting. Changing the names of sections can create confusing archives.

They decided to rotate the position of Administrative Editor every three months, since so many were technically proficient. The first volunteer was a girl from Pakistan. She was a pro at age 13. Noted for a keen sense of humor, she was all business when it came to the JJ and sent out this note on her first day as the "technical boss":

"I'm the Administrative Editor for the Junior Journal for January. It's my job to set up accounts for new members in PLUTO (the software that we journalists use to put together our JJ), see to the technicalities in the JJ, answer any Qs you may have, and basically help you use the software.

"So if any of the new members of the JJ taskforce would like to have an account in Pluto and learn how to use it, please contact me!"

Could they pull it off by January 1? No problem, they all said, not realizing that the technical details are especially daunting for a first edition. They were undaunted.

By now, December already was ticking away, so on Dec. 8 I sent out a more detailed summation of where they were at with more close-to-the-bone questions designed to prompt necessary decisions: Who was going to write what? Did the 20th day of the month make sense as a deadline for submissions? (Deadlines should be clear, as should be the mechanism for granting exceptions when absolutely necessary). How many editors should screen each story (they decided three)? What's the minimum number of stories for an edition (8-10, they said, and in later issues they had 70 stories on several occasions!)? How long (300-400 words on average)? Can non-delegates write (definitely)? Should one editor be in charge of each section (no)? They also asked me to choose the first editor just to get things started (I picked a name out of a hat). They were fast and decisive.

It was amazing given the fact that other groups have spent at least two or three months in similar preparation, because 90 percent of the decisions made for the first edition won't need to be revisited in subsequent editions.

Down to Basics

Just as an example, here is a distillation of some of the technical tasks the Rye group put together in a progress memo a week before publishing:

- Decide font, size, color of masthead (also a photo to go with it).
- Fix up line under masthead and decide on wording ("Published by . . .", date, etc.), type size, "heaviness" of rules top & bottom.
- Decide size of section headings
- Decide where to place a Feedback link and a place for members to log in.
- Volume numbers? (Decided they didn't need them).
- Design the front so viewer won't have to scroll too far to get to the bottom of the page; avoid a page that's too busy; add helpful links; decide on color, style harmony; create a legal statement linked from the Copyright line;[1] make copies of all templates and be sure to file.

It was Rye's turn for a startup in 2005. Juliette Zivic hadn't used HTML for several years, so a month before the first Rye edition she and her husband, Martin, a retired engineer, set out to re-learn HTML. They volunteered to be co-Administrative Editors with her handling publication of the first edition. She painstakingly created the first edition offline so she could test out things such as sizes and colors and photo placement. Converting it all online was even more difficult, because the software used both HTML and Scheme. Somehow she managed it.

John Averell of the Melrose SilverStringers made himself available for the two weeks leading up to publication and was kept busy answering questions. Again it proved the priceless value of linkages among groups. Included in Averell's many contributions was a one-page at-a-glance "Introduction to your PC" that he put together.

It read as follows:

WINDOWS operating system: 95, 98, ME, XP, NT
[Mac/Apple operating system not covered here.]

Power to your computer
Starting: first all peripherals, last the computer (CPU)
        Wait for system to finish starting. May take awhile. May need login
Stopping: NEVER turn off power switch while computer desktop is showing.
        Mouse: Start/Shutdown
        Keyboard: Ctrl+Alt+Delete

Keyboard
        Ordinary keys, Shift, Ctrl, Alt, F1-12

Monitor
        desktop, icons, toolbar

Mouse (2 buttons at least)
        cursor
        click, double-click, press, drag
        left – mostly used, click=focus and button activate, double-click=start, press for drag & drop
        right – press=drops down menu & select item

Toolbar – bottom of screen
        Start button – Programs, Shut Down (and restart)
        Quick launch icons – single click
        Running windows icons – restore minimized programs
        tray icons – always running – connections, anti-virus, sound, IM, clock

Window – All programs displayed in a window
        top strip – right-click=minimize, maximize, close
        lower right – resize window
        menu bar – File, Edit, View, . . . Help
        toolbar – various tools
        (browser) address bar

Internet – have to be connected
>   Service provider – paid. AOL, Juno, PeoplePC, Comcast, RCN
>   telephone dialup modem – ties up phone, slower, login password
>   cable modem – no phone, fast, always on

Email
>   may be provided by service provider (Comcast, RCN)
>   may be separate and accessible with browser (Hotmail, Yahoo, MSN)
>   may be separate email program (Outlook Express)

Antivirus – EVERYONE SHOULD HAVE AN ANTIVIRUS PROGRAM
INSTALLED AND UPDATED SEVERAL TIMES A WEEK.
>   Norton (Symantec), McAfee, . . .

Internet Browser – the interface with the internet.
>   Internet Explorer – included in all Windows operating systems.
>   Separate from Service Provider
>   Other browser (Mozilla Firefox, Netscape, Opera, . . .)
>   Also provided by Service Provider (AOL, Earthlink, PeoplePC, . . .)
>   *URL* – the internet address. http://www.something.com

(Averell, a PhD who worked at Avco, Lotus and Polaroid for 19 years, would have been an outstanding professor. He had joined the SilverStringers soon after retiring in 2000).

For the first Rye edition I did most of the insertion of coding within stories for photos and artwork, mostly learning by trial and error as I went along. It was agreed that I would publish all the stories within the sections, and Juliette Zivic, in a separate follow-up procedure, would publish the front page. I decided no one would know the difference if I published a day early. Juliette independently decided to test her work by publishing the front page a day early. Suddenly we were on the internet on June 1 carrying a publishing date of June 2. She joked that it was already June 2 in New Zealand. In truth, neither one of us dared unpublish for fear we wouldn't be able to republish. Besides, it looked pretty good. Better to be early than not at all.

CHAPTER FOUR

The Community Dynamic

"I note the obvious differences
between each sort and type,
but we are more alike, my
friends, than we are unalike.
We are more alike, my friends,
than we are unalike."

Maya Angelou in *"Human Family"*

COMMUNITY GROUPS THAT live by rules tend to die by rules. Guidelines are a better approach, and even they should be kept flexible and to a minimum. That said, who runs the show? How are meetings conducted? Who decides what chores have to be handled and who handles them? What's the mission? Who can be a member?

The short answer: One formula doesn't fit all. Yet there are more similarities in the group dynamic than dissimilarities. Take membership as an example.

It's one thing to say everyone is welcome, no questions asked, when you are part of a physical community. It's wholly different when you are children or teenagers in a widely dispersed community, such as was the case with the Junior Journal. Yet the Journal editors were uncanny when it came to screening newcomers. They kept their left hand high to avoid being infiltrated by an adult posing as a child or to prevent commercial interests from taking advantage of them in some way. Having a network of members in so many countries enabled them to do reference checking.

A girl from Argentina was anxious to write for the Junior Journal and received the standard answer when she contacted the editors: The Journal needed verification that she was under age 19. Within an hour they received an email from her with copies of the front and back of her identity card, showing her photograph and her date of birth (she was 18). They were so impressed with her fast response that they allowed her to write her first article in Spanish "to encourage her". Articles in the Junior Journal were generally in English, but the editors occasionally made an exception if someone wrote in only French or Spanish. A few times the articles were run in both languages.

After her first article appeared, one of the editors, Spiros Tzelepis of Greece, wrote her a congratulatory note and asked if she would like to try writing in English. "I explained to her that English is a second language for me, too, and that I make a lot of mistakes, too." She responded with an article in English for the next edition and several more after that. Her writing, mostly about cinema, improved with each offering. Later she wrote to say, "This is one of the most beautiful experiences in my life, and I am really proud of being part of it."

In 2003 a request to have an article published was received by the Junior Journal from someone with a girl's name. After close questioning via email the editors determined that it was a woman, who ran a company that did interviews and profiles of "progressive teenagers around the world." Hmmm. They rejected her offer.

Even with strict monitoring, Journal editors knew there was no foolproof way of knowing who wrote stories being submitted. One editor wisely observed: "It is of no use for them to pretend to be someone else . . . because in the end they cheat themselves."

Limitations Generally Avoided

Age often is used as a standard for membership, usually with built-in exceptions. The Junior Journal set ages 10 to 19 as its standard but once ran an article by an 8-year-old and another time carried a front-page photo by a 7-year-old. The Rye Surfers described themselves as being open to anyone over 50 years old, then agreed it was an artificial barrier. In the first issue they referred to themselves as being "produced and directed by an adult group", only for the purpose of differentiating themselves from a youth venture being planned in their town. Melrose avoided the age number altogether and has come up with a set of guidelines that carefully set parameters but avoid the strait-jacket danger:

SilverStringer Guidelines

Purpose of SilverStringers:

The primary purpose of the S/S is to provide a technical and organizational means for Melrose seniors to publish an internet journal, the Melrose Mirror, containing articles and photographs of general interest.

Secondarily, the regular meetings of the S/S provide a way to exchange ideas and information in a social setting, which will serve to encourage participation of members to contribute to the Melrose Mirror.

Who can be a member:

S/S is by its formation primarily an organization of seniors who have some connection with Melrose, either by present or former residence, or through family ties to Melrose. There is no firm age requirement for seniors.

Members are encouraged, and expected as able, to attend regular meetings.

Members are expected to contribute articles to the Mirror.

Who can be a contributor:

Besides members, there are a number of individuals who contribute articles pertaining to Melrose on an occasional basis from all over the USA, and even the world. The only requirement is that the article is "publishable."

What is a publishable article:

Not all articles submitted are considered "publishable." Purely fictional prose is not acceptable. Acceptable articles are news, feature stories, essays, poems, informational notes, letters about articles, photos with accompanying text to bind them into a presentation, memories, current events pertinent to Melrose . . .

Purpose of Editors/Publisher:

The editors are a group of members whose task is to review submitted articles for suitability, correctness of grammar and spelling, and if necessary, to interact with the author where suggestions of substantive changes are recommended.

Editors' decisions may be appealed to the members for recourse and a final decision.

The editors are expected to add any technical text to the articles necessary to display photos in a pleasing way.

The editors present to the publisher (who is one of the editors on a rotating basis) articles that are deemed suitable for publication, conform to standard format, are free from textual errors, and whose appearance on the internet will be pleasing.

The publisher makes the choice of articles and photos for an issue, and is responsible, with the concurrence of the editors, for publishing the current issue of the Mirror on the internet.

Who can be an editor:

Editors should be members who: actively attend regular and editorial board meetings; contribute articles to the Mirror; have access to a computer and are able to login to the Mirror and edit articles submitted to the editors.

Submitting articles/photos:

Articles may be submitted by members directly online, if possible.

Articles may be submitted in hard copy to an editor (or any willing member) to be submitted online.

Photos may be submitted to accompany articles directly online if possible, or in digital form, or in print form to be scanned and digitized, by any willing member.

Deadlines on submissions:

Articles must be submitted by the Friday preceding publication date. Photos should accompany articles if possible.

Under extraordinary circumstances the editors may accept articles after the normal deadline.

Format of articles:

Articles in the Mirror have a title, an author, a summary, and a body.

Title: First word and proper nouns capitalized, otherwise lowercase.

Author: by [your name] for example, by John Jones use default article template
    if submitted for someone, from [name] for example, from Mary Smith use without-author-link template

Summary: a space, three dots, space, then short summary in lowercase. for example, . . . a message to President George Bush

Body: One space only after period. Two Enters for paragraph (i.e. a blank line between paragraphs.)

HTML tags as appropriate may be added by editors.

In one document the SilverStringers have touched on operational guidelines as well as a few style issues. What are not stated are customs and practices – and tools – that have developed over time. Tools, you ask? O yes. Early meetings were conducted with a set of tools that included a wooden mallet and an hourglass. When the meeting got out of order, usually because of too many side conversations, the chairperson whacked the meeting table with the mallet. That got their attention. When someone talked too long, the chairperson would pull out the 60-second hourglass and set it on the table in full view. The hint usually got across, and those particular tools were no longer needed after a period time. But there is one other tool they still use: The alphabet. It is used to determine who is chairperson. The position is rotated alphabetically with each person responsible for running two meetings in a row (the Rye group has found rotation to its liking as well).

The role of the chairperson is to:

- Call the meeting to order
- Circulate an agenda for the meeting.
- Introduce any new members (if there are any, the veteran members then introduce themselves)
- Ask each person if there is one item he or she wishes to mention (often there is more than one, and no one squawks if it doesn't take too much time).
- Call for a reading of the minutes of the previous week's meeting. **Tip: Archived minutes are vital, especially as a record of policy decisions the group makes.**
- Review what stories and photos are being planned for the next edition.
- Open discussion for new story/photo/art ideas.
- Introduce the topic or discussion item for that week.

Kay McCarte speaks as part of a SilverStringers presentation at national AARP convention in 2007.

Special Attention for Newcomers

Rotating duties is a way of sharing the few burdens there are as well as giving everyone a sense of belonging. The secretary or minutes-taker role requires someone who has a good attendance record and takes notes well. Some groups have a designated greeter to be sure any newcomer who wanders into a meeting is given a suitable welcome and description of how the group functions. Sometimes a treasurer is needed to handle small contributions for get-well or sympathy cards or to fund the annual party. Melrose always celebrates its birthday with tongue-in-cheek skits followed by refreshments. They request $5 contributions but don't keep track of who donates or who doesn't. (Groups with non-profit websites, of course, don't have the business concerns of for-profit sites that carry advertising).

Occasional social activities tend to bring groups closer together.

A greeter not only helps a newcomer feel comfortable but also provides a mechanism for orienting that person. The Junior Journal used the Administrative Editor to handle that function. The "AdminEd", as they called it, gave out passwords, provided instructions on how to use the system, spelled out what the deadlines were and what was expected of the participants. Any group materials that are in writing should also be made available. Many groups put together something called Frequently Asked Questions or FAQs for new members. The Junior Journal AdminEd played a strong role but also understood the need for consultation, again, all done by email. Here's a simple, unedited example of how that worked when the AdminEd put together a form letter that was passed by the other editors:

> *Hi everyone,*
>
> *Here's the standard letter I came up with. The stuff in the brackets <> is meant to be read by you ... tell me if its OK, and if any corrections need to be made. I tried to make it as friendly and open-minded as is possible, 'cuz after all the JJ is a global children's newspaper, a medium through which kids all over the world, JRS participants and non-JRS participants alike, should be able to express their views and ideas. I agree with Mary and Hilary that we need to be warm and welcoming to the people who write to us, and not too formal.*
>
> *Anyway, here it is:*
>
> *Dear <name of person, if given. otherwise, 'friend' is OK>,*
>
> *Hi! Thanks for writing to the Junior Journal. Hope you enjoyed browsing through our newspaper. If you want any more information about it you can check out http://journal.jrsummit.net:8000/faq.htm <should we include this FAQ part?>*
>
> *As the Junior Journal is a relatively new publication, we try to choose our reporters and journalists from among Junior Summit participants <when we say 'the outside world', it sounds a bit, well, alienish, don't u think?>. However, you're welcome to send us any article you have written, which you feel is on a topic worth*

thinking about. You can send your articles along with your particulars (Name, Age and Country) to one of the Editors to be checked and edited. But access to the special program used by us Junior Journalists to create the newspaper is restricted only to Junior Summit participants.

If you are interested in writing for the newspaper, please don't hesitate to contact us at <what e-mail address should we use for this purpose?>
Thanks!
Always,
<who should the letter be sent by? all the editors or just me?> The final letter had few changes, other than the necessary editing.

Fiction Presents Difficulties

New members often are oblivious to certain basics that "veterans" take for granted. At least a dozen times I have done presentations to groups on how to get a story idea, but it wasn't until 10 years into community publishing that I realized few knew precisely what was meant by the word "story". And so, when I started off with the Rye group, I handed out a basic list of story categories that seemed to help a lot.

NEWS:
Live Events
    Coverage
    Reaction
    Analysis
    Mood reflection
    Reader surveys
Interview
Issue story
Trend story
Police/Fire/Crime
Consumer information (managing money, dragonflies)
Deaths/Appreciations/Obituaries
Weather/Storms
Previews of coming events
Government/politics
Business
School activities

FEATURES:
Profiles of individuals
Profiles of institutions/organizations/businesses

Memories
Reviews (Selectman's meeting or music, books, plays, movies, art exhibits, flower shows)
Travel
How-to stories (bring up children, build a shed, etc.)
Personal experience (growing up, moving, grandparenting)
Problem solving (serious/humorous)
Relationships
Learning
Reflections on holidays, time of year, event anniversaries
Hobbies, games
Humor
Automobiles/Airplanes/Boats
Animals
Health/Medicine
Genealogy
Entertainment
Food/Cooking
Local architecture
Spectator Sports

Participatory sports (Hunting, Fishing, Bowling, etc.)
Science/Nature/Outdoors
Culture/Rituals/Religion
Sex/Drugs/Rock 'n Roll
Social Issues
Technology
Natural phenomenon (pond, nearby mountain, waterfall)

OPINION
Group editorial
Personal column
Satire or humor column

POETRY

Groups can decide for themselves, of course, but they generally rule out fiction for use in a community "magazine" or "newspaper", because (1) they'll likely get swamped by manuscripts people have had stashed in a bottom drawer for years and because (2) the editing requires expertise that is more specialized than what's needed for news and features and because (3) readers so far haven't found long pieces of fiction on the web appealing. Allowance should be made, however, for an occasional short piece of fiction or tongue-in-cheek story. In the second Rye issue a retired auto dealer courageously tried his hand at writing a humorous story from the viewpoint of a frog, leaping off (no pun intended) from a local controversy surrounding an annual Fourth of July children's frog-jumping contest that some considered cruel and wanted halted. He pulled it off nicely and even used Adobe Photoshop to design a first-place medal that he draped around the neck of an actual frog he had taken a photograph of.

That was a pre-cursor for a regular Rye Reflections sub-section of satire called "Wry".

Need to Pass On Experiences

Veterans of community journalism, of which there are few so far, should be encouraged to capture in writing what they have learned about performing certain functions for the edification of those who come later. These helpful hints can be revised as the group matures.

Deepika Pereira of the United Arab Emirates was 15 when she became a Junior Journal editor (it was no surprise that she later was smart enough to graduate from the University of Wisconsin). After being an Edition Editor for a year or so, she decided to share what she learned with other editors:

> *Hi everyone,*
>
> *Here is a list of duties for the Edition Editor, based on the experience we have had so far. I thought it might help you out when you are edition editor.*
>
> 1. *First and foremost make sure that you know each and everyone of your reporters, they are the key to the whole setup!! Make a list of all their names and their various duties ... some might be editors, or admin editors or hold other posts even.*
>
> 2. *At the beginning of the month as soon as the new edition has been published or if possible even before, start work ... think up ideas for the articles, ask the staff about their ideas. You need at least one article for each section but try for at least two.*
>
> 3. *Once you've gathered all the possible themes for the articles – some of them yours and some you get from other editors – write them down and send a general message to the editors informing them that these are the ideas and ask who can work on them as well as suggest a few people who might want to do them. Remind them that photos are needed as well.*
>
> 4. *It is actually a good idea to let the reporters work on their own ideas for the articles ... they would be more interested to work on their own suggestions rather than others. And you'll definitely get a better output. So when assigning someone to an article always ask them if they have better ideas that they would like to work on instead of what you have suggested.*

5.　*Once all articles are being worked on, you have to make up a list of two editors to each article. Go to the editor's basket "every day", and, if new articles have come in, immediately assign editors to the articles and let them know. Remind them to "Save" and "Preview" the article after they have edited it.*
Here is an example of how the Edition Editor assign editing:
Spyros & Manal=Please edit the Whatever Story (#256).
This would mean that Spyros would edit it first, then send email to Manal letting her know he has finished. He also would write a line in Notes at the end of the story saying something like: "Edited by Spyros, Jan. 24".
After the second editor (Manal) finishes, she also should write a line in Notes saying, "Edited by Manal, Jan. 27," then send the story to the Publishing basket.

6.　*Be organized, keep your list of articles and authors with you at all times, maybe even stick it to the side of your study table or computer desk. Make sure that everyone is working, keep everyone on their toes by sending them personal messages to get updates on how the articles are coming along. This is so that you'll be in touch with what is going on.*
It'll be easier for you.

7.　*Sometimes editors might need help with editions. In case, they are busy with school, etc., you can do the editing yourself. Also, make note of the reporters who are actively participating and those who are not*
(they might be extremely busy with other things), so you can assign those who are busy with a little less work.

8.　*Remind editors about 7 to 8 days in advance that the deadline is the 20th. At about this time you should start to write your "Message from the Edition Editor," because you'll know what will be special about your edition. Another editor should edit what you write.*

9.　*Read all the articles that have come in and make sure they are up to standard. If the article is haphazardly done, then you can politely request the assigning editor to have the author make the necessary changes (suggest some to him/her to make it easier).*

10.　*The week before publication, put a notice on the front page … promoting what's special in the upcoming issue. Something: Coming Aug. 1: a special story on growing rice in the desert. You also should decide at about the same time what photo or artwork you plan to use on Page One, so you don't have to scramble on the last day or so. The photo should be 300 to 350 pixels wide. It can be whatever height you want.*

11.　*Sometimes authors might not want to reveal their names or countries. Talk it over with them and come to some sort of agreement … maybe just the initials or a first name, or just the country would do.*

12. *If you ever have any sort of problem, relax, think about it for a while, listen to "everyone's" opinion on it and then make your decision . . . go with your instincts on how the problem could be solved. If it's a last-minute decision, do what you think will be best.*

13. *Once all the editing is done . . . check each article to make sure that all the content is correct, and it is being sent to the right section. Decide what story will be headlined on the front page. That headline should be linked to the story or photos inside . . .*

14. *Coordinate with the Administrative Editor who will transfer all the articles in the archives on the last day of the month in order to clear out the JJ for all the fresh material. This should be done at a convenient time for both of you, bearing in mind that you often will be operating in different time zones. The Administrative Editor should send you email as soon as everything is cleared out.*

15. *When all that is done, all you've gotta do is sit back, relax and press the "PUBLISH" button which is the easiest thing considering all the hard work . . . it's also the best feeling ever!*
    Deepika :o)
    A pro at age 15!

Style, With Less Rigor

Despite the need to keep written rules to a minimum certain language-usage and type styles need to be agreed to. In the professional world being a stickler for style is applauded, especially if you are a copy editor. In the community-journalism world, adherence is uneven, partly because of the wide range of participant backgrounds and partly because readers of the web tend to be more accepting. Style watchdogs love to pore over newspapers looking for errors in grammar. Or is it pour? In the United Kingdom in 2001, an organization called the Apostrophe Protection Society was formed!

So what are a few of the style issues that need to be attended to?

HEADLINES – Should words be capitalized or should you use downstyle, which most publications have adopted and which follows the same rules as capitalization in a sentence? No period in either case. What typeface should be used (same question for masthead)?

BODY TYPE – What size? What typeface? Should there be two spaces after a period as taught in typing classes or one, which for good reason is the norm on the web? Should each paragraph be indented or start off flush left (if you choose the latter, be sure to have an extra space between paragraphs). How should bylines look?

CAPTIONS – Roman or italic type? Bold or lightface? What typeface? Color? Should photographer credit be at the end of the caption or a separate line under the photo in a different typeface? Should single-line captions be centered or flush left?

After a few basics are decided on – some of which might be somewhat dictated by your software – the easiest route is to make adjustments as you go along. Rye actually had a discussion as to whether there should be two spaces or one after a period at the end of a sentence. Rye's style was two spaces until two years into the publication when it was found that single spaces are more practical. Otherwise blank spaces wind up at the start of some lines and have to be hand-deleted, a tedious process.

The Junior Journal continually ran into problems with spelling (North Americans wrote "color" or "labor"; Europeans, Indians and many Africans wrote "colour" and "labour". The word "maths" is widely accepted in Europe). So the JJ adopted the Economist of London Style Guide, a truncated, but excellent version of its hardcover book.

Consistent style has its place, but passion remains the crucial element in community journalism groups.

New York author Tom Wolfe, probably best known for his novel, "The Bonfire of the Vanities," told a story to U.S. editors in 1990 that should give pause to those who get too carried away with the technicalities of publishing. Here is a summarized form, stripped of Wolfe's storytelling prowess, let alone his sartorial style.

It seems that Time Magazine invited a Zen Buddhist abbot to a luncheon in the executive dining room one day. Most of the discussion was carried by the Time executives, who explained how their massive operation functioned around the world.

Asked at the end if he had any questions for them, the little monk responded, "Yes, why do you publish it?"

Wolfe describes the scene as the editors, "making imaginary snow balls, stammered about responsibility, duty, shedding light on truth, doing it for the good of the people . . ."

At that point, the abbot said, "Yes, but good for what?"

When the question is asked of those who take part in community journalism, no one turns to the making of imaginary snowballs. The answer is crystal clear: It's invigorating.

The following is a sample of a Rye agenda:

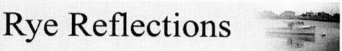

Rye Reflections

Surfers' **AGENDA** January 17, 2008
Chair: Bill Drew

FEBRUARY 2008 ISSUE   Jan 31st deadline; Feb 6th publish

Around the Table Discussion:
- §

Features:
- § Computer Series, Part 6G (A.Harper)*
- § North Hampton, or, Australian Outback (B.Warren)
- § NH State Parks (Drew)
- § Reading, writing, and arithmetic in the good old days (J.Cerny)*
- § World's smallest racing dinghy: the Cape Cod Frosty (J.Cerny)
- § Carbon Challenge (Denise Blaha)
- § It's a Dog's World (H.McFarland)
- § Umbrellas (J.Palm)

News:
- § Rye Crisp (J.Driscoll). *Rotary Club Polar Bear Swim (jwc)*.
- § Toumas interview on HHS on 1/28 (J.Driscoll)
- § Rye Town Meeting Feb. 2nd (J.Driscoll)

Recipes:
- § Anadama Bread (M. Dunn)
- § Strawberries (M.Carroll)
- § Red Velvet Cake (J.Palm)

Poetry:
- § Winter: Jenness Beach (N.Walker)*

Travel:
- § Jackson Hole skiing (B.Dunn)
- § New Year's Eve in London (K.Palm & J.Palm)

Opinion:
- §

Other Items:
- § Hits counters (Harper)

Looking Ahead to March:
Pictures of Paris (Palms); North Hampton/Rye (B.Warren); Juvenile Adventures Stories in Seacoast (J.Cerny); Beach Walkers (N.Walker)

CHAPTER FIVE

The Unseen Benefits

The Unseen Benefits

> *"Community service speaks to me.*
> *It's an integral part of my life.*
> *What I've learned is that it's good for the*
> *body – and good for the soul."*

Jim Parkel, president of AARP,
in May 2002 AARP Bulletin

THEY TEND TO use big words in academia: Such as "plasticity". They also tend to look at the big picture: Such as trying to answer the "why" question (rather than just addressing the journalist's who, what, when, where and how).

A prime example of a book pertinent to community journalism that answers the "why" question is "Keep Your Brain Young". The book is devoted in part to a 10-year study of 3000 individuals between ages 70 and 80. Those in a group of 1200 were found to thrive because of active engagement of their brains as compared with another group of 1800 who were less mentally active. More dramatic was the finding that, with some physical activity mixed in, the brain actually was altered among the 1200, and they lived an average of five years longer.

That brings us to plasticity and the big picture, and it especially brings us to the SilverStringers and other senior groups engaged in community journalism. The book was co-authored by Dr. Marilyn Albert, then of Harvard Medical School, and Dr. Guy Khann of Johns Hopkins University. The study, originally published in the "Psychology and Aging", was sponsored by the MacArthur Foundation and involved 15 U.S. scientists, with Dr. Albert as the principal investigator.

The dictionary defines plasticity as "the capacity for being molded or altered." It is a theory around which major brain research is now being designed to improve physical and mental well-being, combat disease and illness and promote longevity.

Surely community journalism has big-picture benefits to the public as a whole and to the participants themselves. But resultant plasticity adds an even more compelling dimension to the mix. It's pretty simple: Join a group, have fun, experience self-fulfillment, add years to your life.

Publishing's Powerful Impact

What's all this do for the younger generation? Assumedly their active engagement can have an effect on their longevity, but a couple of encouraging studies of the Junior Journal and its participants also are worth note.

They suggest loudly that publishing by children and teens online has positive, powerful impact on social growth, learning and the formation of values.

One research project analyzed four years of email from two lists – the first involving editors and the other all staff member. It was done by Joan Morris DiMicco (now Dr. DiMicco) of the MIT Media Lab and is entitled: "The Junior Journal: An Analysis of an Adolescent On-line Social Network." The other was a 10-month story-by-story case study of moral values by a Pepperdine University class under the direction of J. Lynn Reynolds, an Assistant Professor at Pepperdine University, and Sarah Hock, a lecturer at Santa Barbara City College.

DiMicco pored over more than 3000 pieces of email in what is known as an ethnographic analysis. She wanted to explore how an email-based children's community would evolve as a social network and how decision-making would be approached. She concluded that the participants "flourished" and that they were driven by an interest in "the public good" to arrive at decisions after sometimes rancorous debate.

She also found that they develop the kind of social skills needed for eventual participation in adult society, pointing to the work of John Cotterell who maintains that the development of personal identity is paramount among adolescents. "Participating in an organized group helps a teenager feel accepted and recognized for his/her individual abilities, and with that comes a feeling of pride and a public association with that group," she wrote, again expanding on Cotterell.

DiMicco cited some of the simple procedures adopted by the editors as contributing to positive relationships. One of them involved a series of tests newcomers had to go through to move up to an editor position. "These tests are not seen as exclusionary, but rather as rites of passage and a sign of successful participation," she wrote. The tests involved the need to have contributed regular submissions of stories, participation in online discussion and a stated willingness to devote the time that would be needed to be an editor, especially toward the end of each month.

DiMicco implied – and I think she was right – that the Junior Journal community suffered from a lack of face-to-face contact. Some had met in person at the Junior Summit and developed strong friendships. She suggested that the custom of rotating responsibilities, such as having a different edition editor each month, helped in bonding them. Future international publications, whether involving teens or adults, would benefit from in-person gatherings every few years. It helps charge batteries and is a way of more easily integrating newcomers.

Finally, DiMicco spent considerable time on the decision-making process, which she saw as a mechanism that ensured their long-term survival. "When decisions did not flow so smoothly, which was most of the time, there would be considerable debate on the topic, which could extend for weeks. Yet, their policy stood that even if people disagreed, they would agree to disagree, and accept the majority's decision . . . this did not prevent or discourage disagreement in the group."

Hope a Key Virtue

The Pepperdine study also has relevance that stretches well beyond the Junior Journal, because, as it points out, most education research on moral development has resulted from classroom observations. Yet the internet is playing a bigger and bigger role in learning inside and outside the class setting.

Researchers studied 206 articles over a 10-month period in 1999, using a qualitative method called "close reading", which involved analyzing paragraph by paragraph and sentence by sentence for possible themes. The main theme that emerged was "a belief among the children themselves that they can change the world if they work together."

This work was based on the Moral Act Theory whose author Richard T. Knowles focused on hope, will, purpose, competence and fidelity as key virtues. The Pepperdine study chose a poem by Nusrah Wali, 16, of Morocco in the May, 1999, edition as being reflective of all five virtues. It read as follows:

Who are we?
We live, We breath, We eat, We sleep.
We are children living in a labryinth
A world of politics
Based on fear
Based on hope

We feel in our hearts the pain of a friend
We see in our minds the trouble of a nation
We want to reach out
Because we care.

What makes us different from the next person?
The way we think
The way we act
Our open minds.

We have learnt:
Our strengths
Our weaknesses
Our joys and sorrows.

Our Big problem
Is how to help
How to reach to those that need us
How to find
A way
A solution
How to lead them back to peace
How to tell them they are safe.

This is not what we are
But who we are
And what we are trying to achieve.

Knowles' theory sees hope as the most fundamental virtue, prompting the researchers to pluck out several examples. One came from Sasha Galetsky, 14, of the Ukraine, who wrote an open letter in April to "Leaders of the World" in which she said in one paragraph:

"Today, thanks to modern communications technologies, we children from around the world have the opportunity to discuss important issues and solve our problems together. By sharing our personal stories, we have come to know each other better. In spite of our language barriers, different cultures, religions and skin colors, all of us have the same dream: To make our common world better, and to live in peace."

On the virtue of fidelity, described as "the commitment that one makes to a cause" out of moral conviction, researchers cited articles by two teen boys from the Middle East, Lama Jurdy of Lebanon and Victor Gershgorn of Israel. Jurdy wrote, " . . . passion that makes a difference has to come from youth . . . commitment coming from the young is usually unconditional, unlimited and long-lasting." Gershgorn pleaded, "I as a youth am asking you to help me change the area that I live in to be a better place. Help me and my area to build a better future. We all can. YOU can."

The Pepperdine authors had the wisdom to wind up their report by quoting one sentence from one of the most remarkable pieces that appeared in the Junior Journal. The sentence reads, "Why live in the shadow of history, when we can create tomorrow's history."

These were not idle words. They were written with heartfelt passion.

India, Pakistan Teens Collaborate

The story was about Kashmir, the region so hotly contested by India and Pakistan for so many years. Someone on the Journal mail list suggested innocently enough that a story should be done on Kashmir. After all, the JJ had taken on just about every raw-nerve story that wiggled from Bosnia to the Middle East to the first Gulf War to AIDS, child labor and teen sex. The idea set off quite an email exchange, lasting several days. At some point Manal Ahmad of Pakistan and Maitreyi Doshi of India called a halt to the heated words by suggesting that they write a double-bylined article on the disputed land. This was remarkable in itself since they came from the two countries most at loggerheads over Kashmir. Somehow Manal and Maitreyi not only were able to agree on how such a story would read, but they took the adults from both countries to the woodshed in the process.

"What they don't realize is that what they are destroying is not simply land and equipment," they wrote. "It is the entire future of the youth. Our future depends on the consequences of this aged battle over the state of Jammu and Kashmir: either a bright, friendly, peaceful future or a dark, broody, quarrelsome future. When will they learn? When will they learn that it is not necessary to resort to war and violent measures even in the severest of situations? And that every problem, every crisis, CAN be solved by peaceful talks and discussions?"

They were just getting up head of steam.

"Instead of fighting why do we not use this same money to develop our nation?" they asked "Why do we not use this money to educate our fellow citizens? Help the starving children? To develop our industry?

"We think we need to think seriously over this. We are waiting for that day to come when we can proudly say: 'Hey, you know, she is my best friend and guess what? She is from Pakistan, and I am from India,' and vice versa. So what? We are like any other friends. The time has come to tell the elders that we do not like this and will never support them in any way if they continue going all the same way."

It should be noted that in their late teens Ahmad and Doshi took active, separate roles in creating continued dialogue on the subject. And it also should be noted that serious conciliatory talks took place soon after that.

Constructionism Breaks From Norm

A question often asked is, "Why does MIT (and the Media Lab) spend so much time working with communities?" The two most obvious answers are (1) altruism and (2) the need to test technology in real-world settings. Both are part of it. A third aspect, which especially pertains to the Media Lab, has to do with the sometimes-controversial education philosophy called "constructionism". It is a theory that cuts across all age groups and all community environments, not just classrooms. And the lab has tested the theory in a variety of ways with literally hundreds of communities.

Prof. Seymour Papert has been been buzzing around MIT and creating a buzz internationally for more than 40 years. Co-founder of the Artificial Intelligence Lab with Prof. Marvin Minsky, he has a yen to see traditional forms of education scrapped. The shorthand definition of what he prescribes is "learn by making", but that's an oversimplification.

A bit of background. Papert worked with developmental psychologist Jean Piaget in Geneva in the late Fifties. Piaget (1886-1980) was drawn to the issue of how children think, evolving a theory called "constructivism", which, also in shorthand, is described as building knowledge structures. Papert took that one step further, honing his theory of "constructionism", an approach that permeates project after project at the Media Lab. It is a departure from the standard classroom approach, which for the most part involves the student as a receptor and then transmitter of information and ideas.

In numerous electronic publishing projects constructionism was a cornerstone. Alan Shaw's neighborhood teens cut their teeth on learning to fix appliances, then graduated to computer repairs. The Junior Journalists took the Media Lab's publishing software and added little modifications here and there as they learned how to manage the program rather than having it manage them. All groups found themselves to be believers of the mantra that says that "the only way to learn how to write is to write." Little did any of us know this was constructionism.

An abstract theory, yes, but its importance traces back again to the fact that learning and the development of critical thinking promote plasticity. They are at the foundation of community journalism, and they are enhanced by group interaction.

Drawing on his training as a mathematician and his ability as a storyteller, Papert has spread his learning philosophy through the years in talks, in experimental projects and in writings, especially three books: "Mindstorms", "The Children's Machine" and "The Connected Family". In "Constructionism", a collection of research papers, Papert provided this definition:

"Constructionism – the N word as opposed to the V word – shares contructivism's view of learning as 'building knowledge structures' through progressive internalization of actions . . . It then adds the idea that this happens especially felicitously in a context where the learner is consciously engaged in constructing a public entity, whether it's a sand castle on the beach or a theory of the universe." Edith S. Ackermann, an educator and science researcher, has done some of the clearest writing about the differences between Piaget's constructivism and Papert's constructionism. In a book chapter she wrote:

"In expressing ideas, or giving them form, we make them tangible and shareable which, in turn, helps shape and sharpen these ideas. Externalizing ideas is also a key to communicating with others. We can only negotiate meaning through tangible forms: our own expressions or existing cultural mediations (language, tools, toys). The cycle of self-directed learning is, to Papert, an iterative process by which learners invent for themselves the very tools and mediations that best support the exploration of intriguing ideas."

A Less Academic View

So that's some of the academic underpinning for community journalism. What follows are a few anecdotes which may seem to trivialize the academic "big picture" but in fact support it.

ON KEEPING THE BRAIN YOUNG – Natalie Thomson has been among the SilverStringers most willing to try her hand at every aspect of journalism. A smooth writer with natural wit, she could have easily churned out readable stories without leaving her computer. Instead Natalie was among the first to do an interview, create a crossword puzzle, cover a live event, go out on a team photo assignment, review a symphony, do a variety of first-person experiential stories and on several occasions write poetry (one of her best was about having a cold and was entitled, "I feel biserable."). In the early days of the Melrose Mirror she arranged an interview with someone at the local coffee shop. At the next meeting she was asked how it went: "I feel like I'm 35 again!" she gushed.

ON SOCIAL NETWORKING – A 12-year-old boy from France sent the following email to the other Junior Journalists: *"Hi! to Everyone! I'd like to tell a little story. A few days after I got home from Cambridge, I saw that the famous singer, Barbara Hendricks, was going to sign her latest album at a store near my house. I wrote her a letter telling her about the Junior Summit and all our work. I then went to the store and bought her albums – I really think that she has a beautiful voice!! – and then got in line so I could have her sign the album and give her the letter. When I got to her, I not only gave her the letter but I also asked if I could kiss her!!! and she let me. Well, I never heard any more from her and had given up hope. But yesterday, guess what? I received a letter from her saying how much she supported our work (unfortunately, she didn't offer any financial aid:-(but I'm writing this for two reasons. First, because there are people out there who are interested in what we're doing and also because she told me in her letter that she has a son, who is very interested in what we are doing . . . So now if we can just continue to think of people to write to, to contact, to let know about what we are doing . . . Bye4now."*

ON MORAL VALUES – Marta Ferreira of Portugal wrote the following October 2001 Junior Journal story, which is shortened slightly in the interest of space:

"I'm in the end of my summer holidays here in Portugal. There was a swimming pool, a beach nearby, a supermarket . . . It was really nice. I went with my granny, granddad, mum, dad, sister and cousin.

"In that place there were a lot of cats. And, of course, there were lady cats, which could be . . . Pregnant! Now, this year, this cat started visiting us. She was really pretty, and she was pregnant. My grandma once gave her milk, so she (the cat!) thought the little patio of our house was a fine restaurant!

"We kind of fell in love with that cat, for she was so nice, so pacific! She let us pat her, and she rubbed against our legs, and purred.

"And we gave her food. We even bought cat food! And we gave her a name: Lili.

"Well, one day, my grandma and granddad came back from the beach early and stayed at my house. My granny was sitting in the patio when Lili came in meowing a lot. She even jumped in her lap, which was very unusual! My granny gave her milk, for she thought Lili was hungry, but Lili just licked it a bit and ran off like mad.

"She didn't come back that day. We started to worry. Where was she? The very next day in the morning, we were all in the patio, when Lili came in, really hungry. We then noticed she wasn't fat. She was NOT pregnant. She had had her babies! So Lili came every day, and she rested in the safety of our patio, and even came in the house. She even brought a friend once, a black cat, that ate too, but was a little scared of us.

"That was cute. We thought that, in some way, Lili had told the other cat that there was food in this house that she could eat there. We all loved her . . . And she loved us, I was sure!

"Then, on the day before we were going to leave, Lili came in as usual, but not very happy. She meowed a lot, which was weird, because she wasn't a cat that meowed a lot. Suddenly, she disappeared. Quite normal. But something that wasn't quite normal happened. Lili came back, bringing a baby in her mouth! A cute baby cat. (Just to prove that Lili was so nice, she let us pick her baby up!) Lili gave her milk, and the baby, with still closed eyes, stayed close to her mother, giving little meows. My father said that she (the baby) had a hurt leg.

"My mum said that the baby probably fell off her 'nest' (we knew where it was, but it was well hidden and high up!) and got hurt. Lili got scared and came to us to ask for help. We didn't go, so she brought the baby to us. She knew that she would get food, love and attention. So she brought the baby to 'safety'. I was quite moved.

"I wanted to take her to Lisbon, back home, but she was a free cat. And we couldn't take the babies, it was too tricky. So we left a note to the new "owners" of the house to treat Lili well. We left a bit of cat food.

"I miss Lili. But my parents say that she probably will have her normal life back, hunting for lizards and bugs to eat . . . Or she'll attract attention from other people.

"Now, what I think we get from this story is that with such simple things, like love, attention and care, we can help so much.

"A pregnant cat. We fed her and saved her the work of hunting. She liked the food we gave her, and us, probably. She felt safe in our patio. We didn't get a prize. We got something better. A friendship. We got confidence. All for food and love.

"Now, with so many starving children and adults, so many destroyed houses, so much lack of food, so much sadness . . . If we – all of us – can help a cat, can't we help the world be a better place? I say yes. LET'S HELP THE WORLD BE A BETTER PLACE!"

(Yes, all caps in computerese is tantamount to shouting. Marta was shouting.).

ON CONSTRUCTIONISM – Jim Driscoll (my oldest brother) had no intention of becoming a community journalist. He had led the campaign to raise the money in Melrose to convert a small estate carriage house into a senior center. When the MIT delegation decided to approach the senior center about a joint venture, Jim set up the meeting and sat in. When the SilverStringers started, Jim attended the early meetings. When Jim's high school class held a reunion, he decided to write about it. His story was published, and he got a lot of compliments. He had never written before, having spent his early adult years in Europe in the Navy, then as a parent of six and a CLU at the John Hancock Insurance Company. Then Jim decided to interview a popular Melrose fixture who held the yard markers at local football games for 57 years. That story really prompted feedback. Soon he was writing regularly. But he also got interested in editing, even though he hardly knew how to use a computer. Not long after and for several years Jim became one of only three editors who learned the publishing routine. He never took any courses, but he was willing to learn by doing and by making errors he learned from. In Papert's words, Jim in his mid-70s and early 80s became a learner "consciously engaged in constructing a public entity."

Now when I hear the word "plasticity", I know exactly what it means, up close and personal.

CHAPTER SIX

Problems & How to Solve Them

``If people put you down enough,
you start to believe it . . . bad
stuff is easier to believe.''

Vivien Ward (Julia Roberts)
in the movie "Pretty Woman"

B ASED ON 30 years of interviewing during which I explicitly asked job candidates at what age they decided to become journalists, it's clear the bug bites early. About 90 percent said they felt drawn to the career sometime between ages 14 and 16.

The romanticized view is that journalism is like the ministry; it's a calling. A more likely explanation is that aspirants turn to journalism, because it offers a little bit of everything: You are teacher, you are a sharer, you are a public servant, you are a creator of words or images, you have the opportunity to pursue a certain kind of subject matter in which you may have intense interest . . .

Judy Underwood's passion is taking pictures of birds, and she didn't miss when an eagle flew overhead.

Community journalists are also drawn by the little-bit-of-everything aspect, but in volunteer groups "fun" is the operative word. That's the compensation. Still, that doesn't mean participation is difficulty-free.

Problems are bound to surface in the building and maintaining of community and maybe more so in the process of publishing. Faced head on and handled well, problems can strengthen the group; given short shrift or "solved" without input from all the key players, they can be harmful.

Neither the young nor the old has a monopoly on occasional contentiousness. Just about every group has one or two thorns. Some hang on, modifying their behavior in most cases; others leave in a huff or drift off.

There's no magic formula for dealing with malcontents. Pushed hard enough, a group will deal with the problem in its own way in its own time, either with a showdown or with a more subtle approach.

Several years ago I took a ten-week adult education class with a friend who later became a successful lawyer. We were being taught how to teach teenagers. For three straight classes a man sat in the front row, window seat, and badgered the teacher with mostly inane questions. She handled them with aplomb, and everyone in the class was just waiting to see how she would ultimately deal with him. But she remained poised and patient. At the start of the third class my friend sat beside the irritant in the front row. After the fourth badgering question my friend raised his hand. Slowly he stood, raising the level of drama, and asked, "What do you do with a student who monopolizes the class's time by asking repeated, totally useless questions just to hear himself speak?" There was polite applause. My friend sat down. The teacher never answered the question. The badgerer never asked another question in the next several weeks and didn't show up for the last two classes.

Small communities seem to know how to iron out ticklish situations.

Building in some problem-solving mechanisms before troubles arise tends to cut down on future bad feelings. Early in its existence the Rye group tackled the question of what to do if the editors turned down a story and the writer disagreed. The question was raised by a person who had taken a risk with a story in the second edition of Rye Reflections. He wrote the story from the perspective of a frog in the annual July 4th frog-jumping contest. It worked well, everyone agreed. But after it was published, he asked: What do we do if a story doesn't "work" in the judgment of the editors, and the writer insists it be published. A healthy discussion of the hypothetical question ensued, and it was agreed that (1) no story would be rejected unless at least two editors deemed it unsuitable, and (2) if the writer persisted, he or she could appeal to the full group.

Melrose has a similar procedure that grew out of an actual rejection and caused some temporary bad feelings. In the Melrose Mirror's first nine years three stories were rejected by the editors' board (the SilverStringers decided the full six-person board had to decide, rather than just two editors). In one case the decision was overturned by the full group.

Some policies have to evolve as situations arise, because you can never anticipate every problem. But there are basics that need to be dealt with:

Who are the editors?

In the early going they usually are members who volunteer.

In the later stages more formal mechanisms for becoming an editor are advisable. They can be voted on by the board of editors or by the full group (Melrose once had a situation in which a member wanted to be an editor but didn't really have the requisite grammatical skills. The board turned him down. He appealed to them. They turned him down. He appealed to the full group. With compassion all but one voted against him).

What are the criteria for being a member? Is age a factor? (The Junior Journal said members had to be between the ages of 10 and 19; otherwise, they argued, they could no longer be referred to as a children's publication). Is geography a factor? (Few require residency)

Being of One Mind in Community

It takes all kinds to produce a publication, professional or otherwise, and diversity of all kinds is a plus. Managing that diversity is a whole other story, particularly in the community form of journalism. Who calls the shots? Who decides, when two persons are at loggerheads over an issue? What about such basic issues as whether or not to publish a hot-potato story as opposed to one that doesn't "work", as described above?

When a dozen persons sit around a conference table, there are a dozen personalities and a dozen opinions on just about every question. The trick is to arrive at a point where the group is of one mind – or as close to one as you can get. To print or not to print is the biggest cutting-edge question, and two controversial Junior Journal stories best illustrate the problem. One was a poem by a teenage girl in the Spring of 2000 and the other was a review in June, 2001, of an Eminem CD with excerpts from "Real Shim Shady", which – you guessed it – were a bit blue.

The poem, entitled "Hateful Fear and Intolerance" concerned classmate harassment and set off a debate that chewed up more than 8000 words of email. The poem read as follows:

A girl and a boy stuck in a crowded classroom.
They have known each other all their lives.
Giving her a dirty look, staring her down with squinty eyes.
They have known each other all their lives,
But he's gonna make the girl take her life.

Make that girl take her life,
Make that girl take her life.

The heat of the hate.
Make the windows sweat
Make the walls mold.

Now all around them.
The students have turned
And they're taking sides,
Watching him.

Make the girl take her life.

Now all the wise guys are in the back.
Making bets.
The one kid says, "I say he's gonna cause a long hospitalization. My money is down and says that he's gonna cause a long hospitalization."

And the other says,
"He's not gonna cause a long hospitalization. He's gonna make that girl take her life.

Make that girl take her life,
Make that girl take her life.
That's where my money is.
So put your money down.

A little while later the teacher steps up.
She sees all the students taking sides.
Sees the wise guys throwing $5 bills back and forth,
And she says, "All right, what's going on?"

And a few of the classmates point to the boy at the back of the row.
She stumbles over the backpacks.
And trips into the notebook.

She sees the boy giving the girl a dirty look.
Staring her down with squinty eyes.
Causing her to take her life.

And the teacher says:
"Why are you making that girl take her life?
Making that girl taker her life,
Making that girl take her life?"

And he says
He says, "That's no girl; that's a dyke!
That's no girl; that's a dyke!
That's no girl; that's a dyke!"
And when she screams, he turns off all the classroom lights.

The edition editor sent out the following note to her fellow editors, framing the debate:

Hi to all the editors ...

What I have here is an article that was written by a girl from my school who has gone through bad times because she's different. It's an article on homosexuality and this article is really powerful but I need your vote on it ... if you think it may be too controversial to put in the JJ then I understand but I believe somebody needs to make people aware of the situation that teens like these go through every day. The highest %age of teens who commit suicides are homosexual. And I think it's very sad ... I think our society needs to accept these people rather than treat them as outcasts. Well, let me me know what you think ASAP

The first response:

"I vote for the poem to be included. I think the article could be enhanced with an article – written by you, or your friend, discussing the problems homosexual youth face – within school, and wider society. Statistics like that on youth suicide are probably good things to include."

"I don't mean to use this article as a means of 'justifying' to our readers why we are publishing the letter (although it might also do that), but simply to make the message more powerful."

Snippets of other responses:

"I am extremely skeptical about this poem and after giving it a lot of thinking I would vote no . . ."

"We cannot choose whether we are homosexual (or otherwise) any more than we can 'choose' to be born male or female . . . Why would someone choose to be homosexual if they were going to be abused, teased, even violently assaulted? (which is what they definitely experience) . . ."

"I do not find any reason to talk about it or promote this difference . . . If we talk about a matter, we magnify it . . ."

"I say go with the poem. Yes maybe it's controversial as our inner debates have shown, but I thought our policy with the JJ was to be pretty open . . ."

"We have to work together as a team . . . it seems like there is sooooo much disagreement here . . . and I really don't think it's good for the paper . . . I want to hear what the rest of the editors have to say."

"I am afraid I cannot agree to publish her article. I know it will to some extent widen the area and variety of our contents, but we have so many things to publish before using this article . . . Also, most of our intended readers are kids . . ."

"I think most articles in JJ 'promote' the author's view, and I think this is good. It shows young people *have* opinions."

"What are we trying to do, become one homogenous newspaper that doesn't write about anything because you can find it somewhere else or because someone doesn't agree with it? I really think we need to open our minds a little bit about the articles we'll let in."

"Sorry I just don't know what to say. I think I will also go for the poem as I feel that we are just giving a message not promoting anything. Bye"

"From my point of view, we shouldn't publish such a highly controversial article. I respect everyone's views but due to this article the JJ is in confusion and there is disunity I don't think that the article deserves all this debating. In my opinion we must avoid such topics . . ."

(change of position). "This time, since the identification of the writer has been clarified, I have no objection to publish the article . . ."

"Topics such as 'Homosexuality' etc. are frowned upon in many countries. It is just the value system: the way blacks have been unfairly treated in the 18th century in US. It may be wrong, but that is the way things are right now. A lot of people in the developing countries are probably even unaware of what it means, and topics such as sexual behaviour etc. are not openly discussed. Hence even in JJ, some people will obviously oppose such an article being printed yet it should be printed because of popular support."

(another change of position). "What I think is that it is reality and everyone should know about it, we can't be 'caring and sympathetic' to people who suffer when we can't see and face what they suffer . . ."

The word "vote" is used from time to time, but none was ever taken. Decisions by numerical vote often result in festering dissension; decisions arrived at by consensus after everyone has had a say tend to gain acceptance, and the group moves on. At the Journal, everyone weighed in, some remained opposed, but all were satisfied they had reached consensus. They decided to publish the poem.

In the case of the Eminem lyrics the debate took two directions. One revolved around the issue of copyright, and the young journalists learned that they would have to have written permission to run all of the lyrics but an excerpt could be run without permission as long as it was restricted to a couple of lines under what is referred to as "the fair-use doctrine" in most countries. The other direction the debate took revolved around printing the sexually graphic words. In the end they voted to publish the review but not use the controversial lyrics, essentially for the reason that some of their readers were only 8 and 9 years old and shouldn't be exposed to such language.

On Being Flexible

Occasionally an individual finds he or she cannot adjust to the give-and-take of community. Perhaps blogging is an option in those cases. Some prefer working under a strong-leader structure or one that invokes Roberts Rules of Order. A longtime military officer in one group could never adjust to having the minutes read without voting on their acceptance. Before he joined, the minutes were never voted on. He was such a valuable member, they decided to change their normal procedure and call for a formal vote each week. Instead of the individual adapting to the group, the group adapted to the individual.

What is it that makes community differ from working in the business world or even being a member of a club or civic association?

Psychology professor and author Barbara Sarason identified three properties of a community in 1974: Its members have a perception of similarity to others in the group; they acknowledge an interdependence among members of the group; and the members feel that they are a part of a larger, dependable and stable structure. Social scientists David W. McMillan and David M. Chavis refined Sarason's definition by emphasizing four main characteristics that distinguish a community:

Membership – members have a feeling of belonging.

Influence – members have a sense that the group matters, that as a group they can make a difference.

Fulfillment – the association with the community must be rewarding for its members. "A strong community is able to fit people together so that people meet each other's needs while they meet their own." Shared values make it possible for communities to provide the necessary balance of priorities to be successful at meeting members' needs.

Emotional connection – in particular, members have a shared history.

Then even later McMillan reformulated the four characteristics as:

Spirit – a setting where we can have connections to others, but where we can be ourselves. There should be a sense of "emotional safety," "boundaries," and a "sense of belonging."

Trust – there should be some sense of order. We know that some in the community have more power than others, but we acknowledge and trust that structure.

Trade – a sense of how members benefit from one another and the community. The ideal is to "transcend score-keeping and . . . enjoy giving for its own sake."

Art – "a shared history that becomes the community's story symbolized in Art."

Advisers Don't Volunteer Advice

A group adviser is probably more important for children's and teen groups, not because young people don't have the brainpower or ability to make decisions, but because they don't have the life experience that can be drawn on by turning to an older person. Adult groups also can benefit from having an adviser, who is either a working professional or someone with journalistic or technical background. How should an adviser interact with a group:

Avoid becoming The Leader.

Respond when called on.

Be patient.

Step in on debates on rare occasions.

Flag severe problems.

Don't get drawn in; let them work out issues.

Don't allow members to open back channels to you (easily done by email)

Critique the product.

A few comments on some of these roles:

PATIENCE – I was one of the first to see the Eminem review with the salty lyrics in the Junior Journal Editors Basket. I was tempted to raise a flag. Instead, I decided to let it play out, knowing the decision could go either way. Hey, it was their publication, not mine. The debate was healthy, everyone learned something from it and the Journal was stronger because of it. If I had interceded up front, an important learning experience for them would have been lost.

STEPPING IN – Again, this probably isn't necessary in an adult group, but when debate gets prolonged and personal, the adviser can bring some sanity to the proceedings. Indeed, you wonder if they are just waiting for you sometimes. There are two approaches: the cold shower and the water drip. The longest, most angry exchange by Journal Journal editors was getting nowhere after about 10 days. I swooped in with a pompous lecture, but I'm sure it was the opening line that had the most impact. The opening line of the lecture:

"I say: Enough."
The debate continued on a higher plane for a couple of days with some apologies

FLAGGING – Libel sometimes lurks in a story when least expected. A Journal writer was recounting the story of teen abuse by a businessman who beat young women who worked for him. In one case he even is alleged to have poisoned one of the girls. She barely survived, but someone reportedly had overheard him plotting to poison her and went to the police who put out an arrest warrant. But the businessman fled the country and never faced trial. The story named the attempted murderer. This not only was a moment for me to intercede and inform the editor that changes would have to be made before publishing the story, but again it also was a teaching moment. Lesson One: A person charged in a warrant is innocent until proved guilty. Lesson Two: The businessman could be libeled even without naming him if enough description was contained in the story that would result in a number of people knowing who was being referred to. As a practical matter (as lawyers love to say), it was unlikely the Journal would have been sued – and they had no assets – but it was a situation that required adviser intervention.

BACK CHANNELS – Here's an email I received from a Junior Journalist:

I really did not want to get into this argument so I am sending my views only to you * * * Please keep this to your self. I want your advise (sic) if I should send it to the whole group or not."
Obviously an adviser should never fall into the trap of "conversing" outside channels. It's not good for the members of the groups and can destroy the delicate

trust so important to a group. Additionally the adviser needs to push back when someone goes this route, telling him (a boy in this case) that it's not appropriate to have outside-channel communications and why.

CRITIQUE – As a mature group the SilverStringers like to have their work critiqued. In fact they demand it. Advisers need to handle newer groups a little more tenderly. Non-professionals are not used to having their work put under a microscope. Critiquing can make them too cautious. If anything, an adviser should be encouraging risk taking. Those willing to experiment often produce memorable content. And the best way to learn is by making mistakes. The word "critique" sends shivers down the spines of some, but that's because they came up in the old school in which critiques meant pounding on your mistakes. The Erik Erikson school stresses affirmation. Positive reinforcement pays greater dividends than nitpicking negativism (sounds like Spiros Agnew) that tends to make creators uptight and prone to repeated errors. Along the those lines B.F. Skinner wrote, "What's wrong with punishments is that they work immediately, but give no long-term results. The responses to punishment are either the urge to escape, to counterattack or a stubborn apathy. These are the bad effects you get in prisons or in schools or wherever punishments are used."

The Rise of Citizen Editors

Some newspapers are now acting on the idea of creating Citizen Editors, who are responsible for organizing citizen journalists in their local area. They are, or can be, advisers as well.

Three university projects helped stimulate the concept. Two came out of Northwestern University's Medill School in the spring of 2004. In one, six graduate students, spurred on by their professor, Rich Gordon, and well-known blogger, Jeff Jarvis of Advance.net, created an experimental citizens' site in Skokie, Ill., called GoSkokie.com. Within five weeks 250 citizens had registered as users, and many were contributing unedited material. In the other, a class developed a plan for a teen site and convinced the Quad-City Times in Davenport, Iowa, to back it. Called "Your Mom" (www.yourmomonline.com), it was run by a professional editor, with two paid interns from the university and about 40 teenagers as contributors. Shortly thereafter the University of Missouri Journalism School initiated MyMissourian.com with students soliciting and editing submissions from mid-Missouri citizens.

The most significant US newspaper-initiated experiments at that time were by a free weekly in Bakersfield, California, and by the Rocky Mountain News, which started 40 neighborhood websites in the spring of 2005 under the umbrella of YourHub.com with one editor overseeing the recruiting and coverage by citizen journalists. The California version is at NorthwestVoice.com.

Time will tell how the linkup of established media and community journalism groups will shake out. The idea of Citizen Editor has merit. What's disturbing now is that some news organizations want to use citizen-produced stories without payment. Not so Korea's OhMyNews, which has a fee structure to deal with the numerous submissions it publishes each day. News organizations should think twice before going the route of publishing citizen stories without compensation.

Philosophically the ideal situation would be to have community-journalism groups that maintain their independence with assistance from the media organizations in such a way that both benefit. The public would be the big winner. The New York Times Foundation has created one useful model for media organizations working with schools that could be extended to teen and adult groups outside the school framework as well. Beginning with the Stuyvesant High School in lower Manhattan, the foundation, headed by ex-editor Jack Rosenthal and using volunteer journalists, worked with the school adviser to train students and help them create an online newspaper. The experience led to the publication of Campus Weblines, which contains pointers on various aspects of journalism.

School websites, with or without professionals assisting, tend to suffer from the top-down syndrome. Headmasters are worried stiff about offensive content. Students as a result are uptight and either become super cautious or take a flyer and do something outrageous. Friction has become common for print newspapers at schools let alone online versions.

The Italy and Brazil models seem to have avoided that pattern with schools publishing under the mantel of Kataweb and Estado. Possibly it is because the schools feel the media companies are sharing some of the responsibility. Given their head, as the Junior Journal proved over six years, the young can be as responsible as their elders.

The media needs to do more experimental in the citizen-journalism realm, not to add to circulation or add to the bottom line. With the public good as the only goal, the question that needs to be resolved is how everyone can best co-exist.

How about a recipe that includes one part independent community-journalism group, one part media news operation and one part liaison person bridging the two with some form of compensation as a binding agent? Stir, but don't mix. Of course, an alternative recipe could call for all to maintain their own independence, co-existing as competitors, friendly or otherwise.

CHAPTER SEVEN

Idea Generation & Development

"Come writers and critics
Who prophesize with your pen
And keep your eyes wide
The chance won't come again ..."

From "The Times They Are A Changin'"
By Bob Dylan, 1964

S O YOU WANT to be a columnist. One time-honored tradition when a column slot becomes open on a newspaper or magazine is to give candidates the opportunity to prove their stuff by writing three sample columns. I never liked the idea. Almost everyone has three good ideas. Good columnists set themselves apart by their ability to come up with new ideas and approaches week in and week out. They know how to separate the wheat from the chaff.

(This is a non-sequitor, but it reminds me of the famous quote by Gov. Adlai Stevenson, who said: "An editor is someone who separates the wheat from the chaff and then publishes the chaff.")

For the most part bloggers and citizen journalists tend to steer away from coverage of "live" news, with the exception of conferences they attend or such major stories as the 2005 tsunamis. Instead citizen journalists concentrate on features, trends, issues and lesser news that percolates under the radar of traditional media.

Citizen journalists sometimes fall into the trap of having one good idea for a story followed by a lot of staring off into space. It's a malady easily cured. Where do ideas come from? Are there ways to generate an endless supply? What are the elements of a good idea? And what are the mechanisms for testing an idea?

Where From?

Good ideas have an inside-out quality. They have to come from inside you but at the same time be relevant to the reader or audience. What interests or excites you? What angers you? What makes you happy/sad? What tweaks curiosity? Chances are the answers to those questions would strike a chord with others.

Susan Trausch was a business writer, a Washington reporter, a feature writer, a columnist and an editorial writer at the Boston Globe. She had so many good ideas that her problem was deciding which to pursue. During an in-house training session Trausch described her approach: "Ideas come from just living and doing the daily battle – standing in line at the bank and always being in the wrong one; spending a day trying to get the funny noise out of the car and discovering it's a tube of lipstick under the seat; living in an apartment with cardboard walls; having your credit card rejected in front of your fellow man. I write about the little annoyances that are big pains, and those are everywhere . . ."

Ideas are everywhere and anywhere. They spill out of your mind when you're chatting, reading a book or watching TV. When you bring your particular perspective and experiences to those ideas, presto, you have a better idea.

Some creative-writing instructors suggest you keep a notepad and pen on your bedstand, because in the middle of the night you sometimes wake up with the darndest, most wonderful ideas. Trouble is, most students get up the next morning and have no idea what the notes meant. Nevertheless, it's useful to carry around a little notebook during your waking hours to capture the brainstorm or the fleeting thought that can be translated into a good story or even part of a story.

Frequently I had lunch with the late Don Murray, the University of New Hampshire professor. He always showed up early and would be found sitting outside or inside the restaurant scribbling away in a loose leaf, ringed notebook. It was his Day Book or journal, a not-uncommon companion for many first-rate writers. In Murray's Day Book were tons of ideas for his books and columns that he jotted down in the course of his meanderings, along with sketches that often depicted ideas. He was a visual thinker.

"My columns usually begin with the ordinary," said Murray. "My eye catches a glint from an insignificant element in my life or the lives of those around me, and I see it suddenly with humor, anger, sadness, amusement, nostalgia, concern – emotion gives it significance."

Take a moment and absorb Murray's underlying lesson. He was the consummate teacher. And what he was suggesting is that you not only distill an idea from the ordinary, but you shape it. You put your own imprint on it. You transform the idea by breathing your own life into it.

The early steps of community journalists often are autobiographical. These writings relate experiences of growing up, of poignant experiences, of lessons learned. At times they seem like entries into a diary, but they often connect with the reader and become illuminating. Your story is my story – different in almost all ways when it comes to the particulars but not when it comes to lessons learned or wisdom accrued. Sometimes the connection is less than obvious. The series of stories of a SilverStringer who was a hobo during the Depression connected with me, not because I had any memory of it (having been born in 1934), but because I was aware my family struggled through that era and, if nothing else, I had an intellectual curiosity about the grassroots impact of the Depression.

My father never read a magazine, newspaper or book – even a novel – without a pen and piece of paper beside him. He was not a writer – although he had the talent, but he was intent on capturing salient pieces of information and ideas. With imagination you can find an endless supply of ideas in whatever situation you find yourself.

Localizing, Augmenting, Spinning Off

A common practice in a newsroom is to find a local angle to a hot national or international story. It's called localizing. Case in point was the above-mentioned tsunami. Since Thailand has become a vacation resort, editors were scouring early wire service reports to find the names of people from their region who were there and, of course, names of deceased. Stories often are done on local servicemen who are overseas, generally based on interviews with their families.

Cross-country bikers dip wheels in ocean, a ritual made more significant by young boy's body-english reaction. (Judy Underwood photo)

Disasters frequently are given short shrift by the media when the incident occurs far away. Sara Elo, a Media Lab graduate student, based her Master's thesis on a computer technique she developed to make such disasters more relevant. She called it PLUM, which stood for Peace, Love and Understanding among Mankind.

One day I came across a three-paragraph story as I was surfing the internet about a flood of the Yangtze River in China. I quickly deployed PLUM, and in a minute it generated a map showing what the extent of the flood would have been had it occurred in the vicinity of MIT, which is alongside the Charles River. Then a list popped up telling of major floods in Cambridge over the past 100 years and what the costs were in lives and property damage. The system provided the population of the flooded community, some of its characteristics and how many citizens of Chinese extraction lived in Cambridge. It told a lot more in a matter of seconds that made the story more understandable.

Without trying to explain how the system works, it simply should be noted that she used a set of statistics and other data to augment the news, to bring it home to the reader. (The use of such an "augmentation" system would be equally fascinating for many business and sports stories.) Using less-complicated approaches, community journalists can likewise augment news by finding local or relevant angles. The practice is sometimes referred to as news spin-offs.

Feature spin-offs often are developed around the calendar. Themes spin off from New Year's Day or Valentine's Day or holidays or the last day of school. We would hope the ideas would be more creative than the perfunctory stories we get on Labor Day that pontificate on why unions are getting stronger or weaker or whatever.

Another technique is called the bottom-drawer approach. You get an idea, you write a note to yourself about it and you file the note in a bottom drawer, possibly in a file folder called story ideas. Soon you will have lots of ideas, so it might be well to organize them. Perhaps you could have a folder for each month. Get an idea that might be better to pursue around Thanksgiving and you tuck it in the November folder. Or you might set up folders based on topics, such as people, government, entertainment, food/recipes . . .

From General to Specific

The Melrose SilverStringers generated numerous ideas by putting themselves through an exercise to analyze their community in the spring of 2005. Members were asked what they would tell a person who was moving to Melrose from Nebraska regarding the attributes and shortcomings of the city. They cited friendliness, lack of industry, homey-ness of downtown, neighbors helping neighbors, good transportation, especially to Boston; sophistication; proximity to sports/educational/cultural activity; reasonable consumer prices; physical layout; lack of highway running through city; strength of fire dept. (rated No. 1 at that time in a regional survey of response times), wealth of social-civic activities; lack of liquor availability (liquor stores disallowed due to local ordinance, although alcohol is allowed in big-enough restaurants), active business community, stable government (mayors keep getting re-elected), diversity of restaurants, Victorian architecture. The next step was to figure out how these concepts could translate into story ideas? Here were some thoughts that were prompted:

FRIENDLY? – Interview members of the Newcomers Club about their experiences.

INDUSTRY – How does Melrose compare with its abutting towns? Compare tax revenues and find out how much Melrose derives from industry as a percentage compared with Malden, Saugus, Wakefield and Stoneham.

THE DOWNTOWN – Having done a lot on that part of town, it was suggested that someone at the Chamber of Commerce might discuss what has been done in the past 10 years to make the downtown more homey and what problems they are trying to overcome (parking, always a concern).

PROXIMITY – How about doing a day in the life of . . . a sports team, a museum or two, a university, a Boston theatre, a Cambridge club from the perspective of the SilverStringers. Possibly working in pairs, they could: attend a Celtics game, tour the Science Museum and/or Museum of Fine Arts, take in a Boston play or ballet, maybe go to a jazz club in Cambridge. With pix.

PRICES – A long story not necessary, but it would be quite a hit with readers if their guess is right that items they can buy in Melrose are cheaper than surrounding towns. No need to buy stuff; simply visit certain stores and do price comparisons of like items.

PHYSICAL LAYOUT/LACK OF HIGHWAY – Interview the head of the Public Works Department and find out details about plowing, cleaning up sand in the spring, clearing culverts.

FIRE DEPT. – Why is the response time so good? How about a Q & A with the chief? Ask lots of questions about equipment, personnel, training, alarm systems, new technology, types of calls for help they respond to (still get cats stuck in trees?), etc.

ACTIVITIES – How about one person (with camera) trying to see how many events he/she can attend in one day in Melrose. Fun story.

BOOZE – Are there any groups or individuals who are hot on this issue, either for or against? A little history would be worthwhile. Are the churches opposed to having one or more liquor stores? Are any liquor suppliers pressuring the mayor or aldermen to relax the "ban"? Or is it a non-issue in which case a humorous approach might be a way to get at the issue, which is a longstanding one in Melrose?

THE MAYOR – What's the history of re-elections? Is voter apathy a factor? Possibly interview someone at the Mass. Municipal Assn. See how Melrose compares with other small cities? Is the low pay a factor in the sense that a person who runs has to be altruistic to want to run? What are other mayors paid? Perks? Also, it would be interesting to analyze past elections: one opponent or many? What vote totals have the incumbents received and by what margins have they won?

RESTAURANT DIVERSITY? – A case for the photo team? Go to each restaurant and ask if you can photograph their specialty, possibly with the chef or owner in the picture. Would make a good photo layout or series.

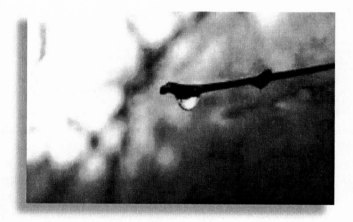

Post-rainstorm "teardrop" captured by SilverStringer Don Norris.

Developing and Testing

Once you get into the habit of writing down ideas for stories as they come to you, the cupboard will never be bare. Now comes the hard part. You've heard the expression, "Ideas are a dime a dozen." It's the development of an idea that's the tricky part and the most important.

This is where community groups are at their best. Lay an idea on the meeting table and let the brainstorming begin. When you invite others to flesh out your idea, it's like turning on a hose. Each new idea triggers another. It's the domino theory in reverse: Instead of knocking down blocks, you are building them. Not all the responses are relevant or worthwhile, but you can't help but wind up with an improved idea.

Story ideas are like loaves of bread. All of the elements need to be brought together and kneaded. Then the dough is popped into the oven until it rises and is ready to eat.

A couple of recommended tests:

1. Examine the idea by writing down a word or two in answer to these questions: Who? What? When? Why? Where? And maybe Why?
2. Analyze the idea based on the following criteria:
3. Does it have timeliness?
4. Is it of importance (affects many)?
5. Will it be of general interest?
6. Is it relevant?
7. Does it involve the public's right to know?
8. Does it involve the public's need to know?
9. Will it inform, educate, guide or entertain readers?

Themes Create Triggers

If worse comes to worse, the best way for a group to force ideas to be generated is to agree on a theme for an upcoming issue. Somehow that exercise seems to induce individuals to focus. The SilverStringers use this technique frequently. Editor Don Norris sent out the following memo on one occasion to force-feed idea generation:

"The theme is to write on current-day mores, customs, habits, attitudes, and behavior – as compared with what it used to be, ah, when we were young(er). This leaves a rather broad purlieu to consider, so the sky is the limit. Say what you want – just make it interesting, informative, biting, astringent, melodious, whatever."

The Junior Journal employed the theme approach for almost every issue, prompting multi-country surveys of such subjects as child labor, child soldiers, the Mideast Conflict, the Gulf Wars, global warming, marriage customs, teen suicide and AIDs.

If all else fails, here's a little idea-sparking drill called "Six Easy Pieces":

1. Where is the most interesting place you have ever been? (Why? What was it like? Describe locale, sound, smells, sights.)
2. Who is the most interesting famous person you ever met? (Why? Explain the circumstances.)
3. In the last six months or so, where is the best place you have eaten. How many times have you eaten there in that period? Before that? (What was served that you liked? How was it cooked, presented, served . . .)

4. What's your favorite TV show? Or, if you prefer, what's the best book you have read in the last year? (Why? Do you recall a particular show? Describe it. Or do you recall a particular part of the book? Describe it.)
5. What political, social or religious issue gets your dander up? (Why? When was the last time the issue got you going? What were the circumstances?)
6. Who was the most significant person in your life who was not a relative? (What was it about that person that you would like to tell the world about?)

If none of the above works, I'm not really sure what you can do. I've run out of ideas.

CHAPTER EIGHT

How to Report

"People who are funny and smart and return phone calls get much better press than people who are just funny and smart."

**Howard Simons,
Managing Editor, Washington Post**

A REPORTER IS an explorer, a searcher, a collector, a puzzle solver, an observer, a conversationalist, an inquisitor, a listener, a schmoozer, a kibitzer, a nitpicker and a stickler, a skeptic, an amateur psychologist, a persuader, a specialist and a generalist all wrapped into one, a squirrel, a bookworm . . . Adjectives that describe a reporter might include curious, bold, tenacious, patient, garrulous, attentive, retentive, industrious, persistent, persevering, purposeful, creative . . . In short, a reporter is multi-dimensional.

Which dimensions should be put into play are determined not by the reporter but by the story being worked on.

I love reporters.

All of the above applies to community reporters as well as professional reporters.

Reporting has two modes: reactive and proactive.

Sixty years ago most general assignment reporters for morning newspapers started their shifts between 3 and 6 p.m. Now they begin between 10 a.m. and 1 p.m.

Earlier deadlines are a factor behind the earlier starting times, but the main reason is story philosophy. The emphasis has shifted from reactive stories to proactive stories. Reactive stories generally come under the heading of breaking news. Yes, they continue to be an integral part of mainstream news coverage, especially for television, but newspapers are more picky about what they respond to. The fire bell, the police siren and the press conference no longer automatically create Pavlovian dogs out of reporters. Proactive reporting requires a different thought process. You are operating less by your wits and more by a well-thought-out plan. You are deciding in advance what story you think needs to be covered rather than just being swept up by events. Often the story content has a broad brush sweep to it, because it is about a trend or an issue. Reactive reporting, it is often said, tends to cover the trees; proactive reporting covers the forest.

Community journalists also tend to be drawn to proactive news – the trend story, the personality, the overriding issue, historic perspective. In media stories about citizen journalists a lot is made of their coverage of breaking news, particularly when the pros fail to show up or when there's a story of immense proportions and citizens jump in, but the preponderance of what community journalists do is the proactive or planned story.

Community journalists have an advantage for most proactive stories. They are better equipped for group-think.

Group photo coverage is an annual exercise for popular Victorian Fair in Melrose. (Photo by Don Norris)

The pace in mainstream media operations is such that story-planning meetings among editors are commonplace, meetings with editors and one or two reporters who will work on the story are infrequent and meetings at which reporters give input to the development of a story another reporter will work on are virtually non-existent. Much of the communication is in verbal shorthand. Deadline pressure is a factor. Newsroom culture is another. Except in unusual situations, such as projects or investigations, large groups of media reporters rarely sit around a table and give input on someone else's story concept.

It can and should happen in community-journalist gatherings, since most such groups meet at least weekly. Time should be set aside for a story idea to be "thrown onto a table" and fleshed out based on the experience or creativity of others in the group. This practice also can occur via email or instant messaging in the case of web publications whose members are in remote locations.

A Junior Journal editor observed that many teen suicides in India were occurring around the time of board exams, so she sent out a note to others on the staff asking:

1. Do such things happen in your country?
2. What do you feel is the reason the students commit suicide?
3. Any solutions you can come up with?

The responses were immediate and resulted in a story that ran in October, 2000. "Here in Hong Kong, students commit suicide not just because of pressure from external exams but also from internal exams because in Primary 6, students who do not do well in school cannot be admitted into 'brand-name' schools . . . remember there was an article written by a friend of mine about stress and the ways to relieve it?? Maybe you could link that to your article. My friend wrote it because she found a way to relieve her stress while having her exams."

In community journalism part of the enjoyment is to lend your expertise to the fleshing out or enrichment of someone's else's story or to be part of a group reporting effort, as was the case in Rye when the 2005 leap in gas prices prompted a how-to-save-energy project with the onset of winter.

The group started out thinking it would do a story with tips on how to save energy for the October issue since that was about the time folks' furnaces would start chugging. In the first discussion there were so many suggestions it was necessary to fine-tune the focus of the story to deal with homespun ideas or steps that weren't widely known. Still, it not only seemed as though it would be an unwieldy story, but the question was raised as to whether the reader could absorb all the suggestions (they ranged from tips on electricity, cooking, basement air leaks, autos, heat, etc.). Finally the group decided to run a half-dozen of the best tips each month during the winter with at least one photo or art illustration.

Not only did the dialogue fine-tune the grand scheme for the story, but it also produced a better way of presenting it.

THE PROCESS: *Stop, Look, Listen*

We've seen so many movies of reporters leaping from their desks, grabbing their hats and suit jackets and racing out the door of the newsroom that we have become accustomed to that popular but mostly inaccurate image. Generally the operative mindset should be, "Look before you leap." The reporter needs to think about what needs to be found out that's new about the story subject. Who would be the best persons to interview? What would be the best questions to ask them? A high percentage of proactive stories involve interviewing.

Still, even before the interviewing phase, there is a need to look before you leap. It's like figuring out where to go swimming in a river. You don't want to just jump in without thinking. You want to size up the situation and find the best spot, where it's not too shallow and not too deep; where boats are unlikely to be buzzing around; where the current is right; where others are nearby (swimming alone is not a good idea).

John Powers converted from being a top-flight Globe sportswriter to being the big-story writer for the Sunday Focus section. Powers and his editor would decide on the subject of his story a week or so in advance, and John would disappear for several hours. He would return with a wire basket full of file-folder envelopes from the library. Each folder had numerous clippings (it's all online now), and Powers would pore through them. He would become an instant expert on the subject of his upcoming story, even before he began traditional reporting.

If you analyze the two parts of the word "report", you will take a giant step toward being a sound fundamental reporter. "Re" means back and "port" means carry. So to report is to carry back. What do you carry back? Answer: specific, accurate information based on what you observe, hear and even feel (such as the rumble under your feet as the truck passes by). Collect facts, impressions, quotations and details. You are carrying this material back to the place where you will write, but more importantly you are ultimately carrying it back to your readers. When you are in the process of reporting, never forget the reader. Try to figure out the questions the reader would want answered. In the end it is the reader to whom you are carrying back all that you collect.

Nota Bene

Assuming you don't have a photographic memory, you can save yourself the trouble of memorizing by taking notes. They save you from looking up a piece of information a second time at a later date. They also help you absorb the information in your mind. It's better to have too many notes than too few. One technique is take careful handwritten notes, then type them as soon as time permits. You might wish to organize notes by subject matter. If time, retyping gives you a better grasp of the material you have gathered. Well-organized research notes translate into easier writing in the end.

Make note when you are taking notes when doing research. Note the name of the book; jot down the name of the publisher and author or authors, the year of publication, what page your notes are taken from. If necessary, make note of any footnotes as well.

If your source is a magazine or newspaper, note the official name (is it New York Times or The New York Times; New Yorker or The New Yorker?); note the author, the date of publication, the page number(s).

Be especially vigilant when researching website material, because the information frequently comes from another source. Clicking on links sometimes leads to the original material. Some web stories list references at the bottom of their stories.

Keeping track of where information comes from can often be as vital as the information itself. For instance, your notes may contain a quotation, saying, "There is only one good, knowledge, and one evil, ignorance." What's most noteworthy about this note is the person you're quoting – the Greek philosopher Socrates.

Then there is the issue of attacking your source material, grabbing it by the neck and squeezing out just the material that's relevant to your story. Say you pick up a textbook with a title something like, "The History of the World". It has more than 1000 pages. It would make a good doorstep. You stare at it and finally say to yourself, "I don't have a clue!"

Where to begin? Get a clue. Rather than starting at Page 1 and reading the entire book, what you want to do is look for clues. The best clues are in the front and in the back of the book. Something called "The Table of Contents" usually is found in the front and contains chapter titles. In the back is the Index, an alphabetical listing of names and words with page references. In some books the Index is thorough; other books only list important names and words. In either case the Index can send you right to the pages you most need to look at.

Photographs often provide valuable clues, too. Sometimes there is a listing of photos in the front of the book with page numbers. Sometimes books are printed with the photos clustered on successive pages. At worst, you might have to flip through the pages to find pictures connected to your research. Occasionally the photographs will lead you to pertinent information because of what they depict or what is mentioned in the caption or because of some information you get visually from the photo.

The Web of Intrigue

Internet search engines are a double-edged sword. They are easy to use but contain the most inaccurate information. It's best to have at least two sources for information that is taken from the internet – making sure one isn't copying from the other.

Take the time to study how best to use these search engines. Sometimes the best results come when you use the fewest words in your query. One of the co-founders of Google, during a Q. and A. period after his talk at the Media Lab, said that three words generally are the optimal number for that search engine.

Use quotation marks around words or phrases that are exactly what you are looking for, such as a name or a phrase. "Old King Cole" without quotes may retrieve more references to Nat King Cole, a popular 20th Century singer, than to the merry old soul.

Let's say you're a little hesitant about a phrase. Was it "one if by land, two if by sea" or "one if by sea, two if by land"? Try both. You'll find neither is correct. It is: "One, if by land, and two, if by sea". Or maybe you know the exact phrase, but you are unsure whether the title is "The Midnight Ride of Paul Revere" or "Paul Revere's Ride". Searching the phrase will quickly tell you the title is the latter.

Take the time to familiarize yourself with the tricks of the search-engine trade. Most have similar rules, but some have tricks or shortcuts that speed your research.

The Art of Kibitzing

Research doesn't always have to entail poring through drawers of file-cabinet folders with moths flying out or slogging through a half-dozen thick encyclopedias.

Human beings sometimes are fountains of information that may never find its way into a library: The 85-year-old who could tell what the Great Depression was like in about 20 states, because he was a hobo; the Irish wood carver whose intricate designs were passed down from his County Meath ancestors; the nurse who worked with Mother Theresa in India; the botanist, the butcher, the baker. Humans enjoy talking about what they are good at or about subjects in which they have expertise. Perhaps you don't want to rely on their information, but they can give you a feel for a subject.

The Tag of Authority

Certain information is common knowledge: The Earth is round, airplanes fly, horses have four legs. Other information is less obvious or may even be controversial (not long ago many believed cholera was caused by "bad air" or "bad moral fiber"). Be sure to make note of "the whom" – the source of your information – when making notes on less obvious or controversial facts.

Here's a piece of information: Modern horses have only one functional toe. It's not common knowledge, certainly is not obvious and even could be controversial. So how do you handle it? You need attribution. You need to answer the question: According to whom?

Be sure your notes reflect the name of the person or other source for any information you collect. Like the antique dealer who needs to be able to tell the customer who previously owned the flower vase, the researcher needs to tell the reader on whose authority a certain statement is made. Not only does name of the original source add to accuracy, but it also helps the reader judge whether the information is believable.

Double Checking

We have established that a researcher is a good advance planner, an explorer, a collector and a keeper of notes about notes and an organizer. We also have suggested that good note-taking avoids the need to look up a piece of information a second time. However, bear in mind that second checking is often a plus and never a minus. The ultimate aim is accuracy. You may be able to remember what year the War of 1812 started, but do you know when the Peloponnesian War began and ended? If you are unsure, even if you looked it up once, double-check it. Double-checking is not a sign of weakness; it is a sign of strength and wisdom.

Editors frequently spout the following: When in doubt, check it out. The need for accuracy cannot be overemphasized. So what causes inaccuracies? Generally the original mistake is made in the research phase and copied in the writing phase. If you jot down a wrong date in your notes, it's likely to be inaccurate when you write.

Care should be taken when it comes to bits of information: the spelling of a name or a person's middle name, a date, a geographic location, a person's exact title, etc.

Usually a second reference can be used as a double-check on factoids: an encyclopedia, a dictionary, Wikipedia, an atlas or book of maps, even a telephone book. When in doubt, check it out. I already said that, you say? Right. And I'll say it again and again. You prefer a shorter version? OK. Never guess!

Once you've done your advance research, the next step for a reporter is to become a dummy, a person who asks dumb questions. Your goal isn't to impress others with your expertise; your goal is to ask questions that will prompt an answer.

How to Conduct an Interview

Interviews, which are best done face to face, have four stages: arrangements, preparation, the actual interview and the reconstruction.

ARRANGEMENTS – Spontaneous interviews, except in connection with breaking news, seldom contribute to thoroughness. Once you have decided to interview someone, **call in advance** to make an appointment. **Identify yourself** by your name and the name of your publication. Provide the URL for your website. If you feel the need to do so or are asked to describe what the story is about, be brief and general. The shape of the story might change as you continue your reporting. If you are interviewing several persons in connection with your story, interview the principal person last, because you will be better prepared based on what you learn from the earlier interviews.

PREPARATION – Do as much **research** as possible in advance on the person and/or topic you are working on, as suggested above. In addition to the library, sources might include the public records, the internet and people you know who can provide background information. Prepare your **questions** in advance in writing and bring them to the interview. Refer to them but don't show them to the interviewee, because it creates too formal an atmosphere. Ask other questions as they might arise, based on what the interviewee says or something new that might come to you on the spur of the moment. Bring two **pencils** (or pens) **and paper**. A stenographer's notebook is usually easier to handle than a large pad but use whatever is comfortable. Bring a **tape recorder** if you can but be sure to get the permission to use it from the person you are interviewing. When using a tape recorder, you also should take notes, because it will help in the reconstruction phase, and, yes, tape recorders fail occasionally.

THE INTERVIEW – It is inadvisable to launch right into the interview unless you are only being given a few minutes. Some casual conversation to start with will relax both of you. Questions should be as **short** as possible. Give the respondent time to answer. Be a good listener. If he or she prattles on, it is appropriate to move on as politely as you can. You might say something such as: "Fine, but let me ask you this . . .". Try to draw out **specifics**: How long, how many, when, etc.? Absorb the **atmospherics** of the locale where the interview takes place, with particular attention to what might be a reflection of the interviewee's personality and interests, such as photos of children or bowling trophies or a paper-littered desk or a clean one, etc. Note **characteristics** of the interviewee that might be worth mentioning in your story, such as pacing, looking out the window to think, hand gestures and the like. Invite the person to call you if she/he thinks of anything pertinent after the interview. It often happens, so be sure to provide your name, email address and phone number on a card or piece of paper before you leave. If that person has a secretary, be sure to get his or her name and telephone number, too, in case there is some detail that needs follow-up and, again, leave information as to how you may be contacted. If a photo is needed and is not taken during the interview, be sure to make arrangements then to have one taken at a later time. Ideally you should bring a digital camera and take the photo yourself. It's preferable to do the photo taking after the interview when your subject is likely to be more relaxed and accepting. Some people just don't like having their picture taken.

RECONSTRUCTION – As soon as it's practical after the interview, find a quiet place to review your handwritten notes. In your haste while taking notes, you may have written abbreviations for words that won't mean anything to you a day or two later. Or some of your scribbling may need deciphering, and, again, it is more likely you'll be better able to understand the scribbles soon after the interview. Underline or put stars alongside quotes that seem most compelling. One star for a good quote, two stars for a very good one, etc. If you don't like stars, come up with your own marking system. It will speed the process when you get to the writing stage. One other thing to look for in your notes: The quote you wrote down might not make a lot of sense, unless you remember what specific question it was responding to. In short, fill in whatever gaps exist in your notes that will help you better understand them when writing.

Details Are Revealing

A bit of expansion on the issues of atmospherics and characteristics that are raised in the above. Your story should carry back to the reader more than just the facts you collect. Words are symbols. You use them to convey to the reader what you've seen, felt, heard, smelled and, yes, maybe even tasted.

A television camera allows the audience to see and hear what the photojournalist chooses to shoot. Word pictures often can go beyond pictures, revealing what the camera might not be able to focus on; describing feelings ("the doorknob was so cold that the skin of your fingers stuck to it") and aromas ("as you walked through the Italian section, the smell of pizza baking made your mouth water").

You are a painter. You are creating a picture that illuminates and even awakens the senses of your readers who might chuckle or grimace or even shed a tear as they not only read but also experience what you are writing. That's why taking note of all the elements of your surroundings when reporting makes sense.

A court stenographer records everything that is said during a trial; a reporter takes notes on the important questions and answers but at the same time is aware of details that may or may not have anything to do with what is being said. When you are interviewing someone, details also can be more revealing than the words that are spoken.

The key to good journalism is context or perspective. Let's examine the difference between a story that results from "emptying your notebook" and a story that flows from "synthesizing" the material you have amassed.

As an example: child literacy. If you did a story on a girl from your community who was illiterate at age 12, it certainly would make a readable story. However, it would also be vital to include other elements, such as: What is the rate of illiteracy in your state or country? How does it compare with worldwide statistics or with countries of similar size or of neighboring states or countries?

Good enough? No, because those statistics wouldn't have much meaning, unless you could give a snapshot of progress or lack of progress. What was illiteracy like ten years ago? Twenty years ago?

Still, statistics don't tell the whole story. Some say there is a tie-in between government funding of education and literacy. Some say there is a close connection between infant mortality and illiteracy. And so on. You need to examine the causes or influences that create a certain effect or outcome. Cause and effect . . .

When you report a story, keep moving your telescope in and out: get the close-up story, the close-in detail, but also draw back and get the big picture. In the end the biggest question you need to answer in your reporting is: Why?

"Couch potatoes" tend to swallow what they see and hear; reporters chew things over.

Getting Interviews in Order

The last thing you want to do if you are writing a story about a person is to interview that person. Literally.

Whether you are writing a profile (that is, a concise biographical sketch) or a story about the exploits of an individual, you should envision your reporting as being like a dart board. At the center is the person you are writing about. The outer circle represents all the written material you can gather about him or her. The other circles can be thought of as containing people who know something about the person. Interview those who know the least first, working your way closer to those who are associates, friends or relatives. Finally you reach your target.

The objective is not to sneak up on the targeted person; rather it is to gather all the information you can, so that you are fully prepared to conduct an informed final interview.

There's another advantage: Time. You don't want to waste time during your interview with mundane questions that you can get answered in advance: How old are you? What jobs have you held? How many brothers and sisters do you have? These questions not only take up valuable interviewing minutes, but they also put the interviewee to sleep. Keep that person awake with sharp, well-thought-out questions and you are more likely to get sharp, well-thought-out answers in return.

Follow this reporting formula, and your story will hit the bull's-eye.

The Virtual Interview

Although most people respond better in person, email and telephone interviewing also have their place in reporting. They are especially useful if you have just a quick question or two, or if the person you wish to interview is too busy to meet with you. Email interviews allow you to send as many questions as you wish whenever you wish. The problem is that you might not get the answers you wanted. They responses may be too short or not quite a response to what you asked.

The advantage of using the telephone for reporting is that you can get a quick response (assuming the person is available to take the call). The disadvantage is that people generally don't have time for a lot of phone questions. If you have more than a couple of questions, the best tactic is to call and ask for a time when you can call back. Give an estimated amount of time it will take. In my experience you should never ask for more than 20 minutes. Otherwise you risk getting turned down altogether.

Letters also can be an effective alternative. They are especially practical when you are trying to do a survey of a group. Newspaper stories on graduations can be boring, because they tend to concentrate on the speech of the boring speaker. At the Globe we decided the graduation day story should be about the class, not the speaker. So we would obtain basic demographic information from the school, then send letters to a large number of students asking them subjective questions (What makes your class different? What was the high point of your schooling? What advice would you give those entering your school? etc.). We would include a self-addressed envelope. All this had to be done about a month before graduation. When the final day came, the survey provided grist for a more compelling story.

The Press Card Fallacy

An explosion on the waterfront . . . United Press sends its rookie (me) to the scene by cab . . . It's 1953, and the Korean Conflict is going on . . . Espionage is the first thought that comes to mind . . . Two soldiers with rifles and long bayonets guard the entrance to the docks . . . Fire and smoke can be seen billowing from an aircraft carrier, the USS Leyte.

"Your identification," says the soldier . . . I don't hesitate . . . Out comes my wallet . . . I show him a card . .." Go ahead!" he says, with a sweeping wave . . . I was first on the scene at an explosion that killed 37 sailors and injured 28 . . . My credentials? A dog-eared union membership card with 12 blocks where stamps were stuck on each month when I paid my dues.

What constitutes a credential? Who certifies the press? Who grants credentials?

In my reporter days in Boston the State Police gave out press badges annually. Later my newspaper said, "Wait a minute! We should decide who our bonafide reporters and photographers are, not a government agency." (The fact that a lot of non-reporters were getting their hands on these press badges was a major factor). So we made up our own badges. The State Police were relieved to shuck the burden.

In controlled societies reporters don't have that luxury. The government licenses them, and that's it. And even in free societies there are instances when badges have to be given out for crowd control or security reasons: covering a country's king, prime minister or president; covering major sports or political events, etc.

Credentials generally are not needed to make appointments or do interviews. Someone who refuses an interview, because you don't have credentials, would probably turn you down anyway. You could make up fancy, laminated press cards for your publication if you wished, but they would be a lot of work, expensive to make (and mail) and impossible to control over time.

So rely on your creativity . . . and your charm.

The Tools of the Trade

Smart reporters are like squirrels: They save nuggets. Sometimes they'll tuck away anecdotes or pieces of information that have nothing to do with the story they are working on, but they hope these nuggets may fit another story on another day. Computers provide a decided advantage. It's easy to store material. The trick is to keep your eye out for snippets of information. Or telling quotations. The "reporting" you do today might come in handy years later.

My computer contains tons of quotes I have kept through the years, and – since you can write till you die – I never know when they might come in handy to help with a story or speech I'm working on. Or just to reflect on. One of my favorites: "Live simply so that others might simply live." Mahatma Gandhi.

The computer has become a reporter's most important tool: Email can set up appointments or ask questions; searches can be done quickly; files can be stored; notes can be easily organized. There also is an advanced reporting technique that some have turned into a useful science called computer-assisted reporting. It is a method by which huge amounts of data can be sorted and analyzed. Several books deal with the topic, so rather than regurgitate, I will defer to those authors, including Prof. Phil Meyer of the University of North Carolina who has given us four editions of "Precision Journalism", and Prof. Lisa C. Miller, who labors in the vineyards of the University of New Hampshire, and wrote "Power Journalism" (Harcourt Brace, 1998).

If you are not computer literate, organizing your notes into file folders is recommended for a complicated story. For years investigative reporters have often used this system as a way of sharing their reporting on a team project. Major newspapers credit the FBI for developing a technique that many adapted. It really came in handy in the late Seventies following the murder of reporter Don Bolles when the Arizona Project was put together. Reporters shuttled in and out of Phoenix over a period of nine months, sometimes for a week at a time and sometimes for much longer, putting together a 56-story series of stories, investigating corruption and malfeasance in Arizona (but not trying to solve the murder).

At the end of each day the reporters would type up their notes in coherent paragraphs as though they were writing a story. Every keyword in their finished notes was underlined in red. If someone's notes, contained 17 underlined words, then 17 copies of those notes would be made and filed under those key words. The files were grouped into major topic areas (drugs, migrant workers, criminal justice system, organized crime, etc.). When it came time, a writer might have available the notes of a dozen reporters on a particular topic to work from. Photos and documents were also carefully filed and cross-referenced.

This is the same system the Globe's Spotlight investigative team used through the years as well.

High and low-technology gadgets of all shapes and sizes, from tape recorders to picture cellphones to Personal Digital Assistants, have become commonplace for most reporters, but stenographer-like notebooks remain a staple. The inside of a used reporter's notebook sometimes looks like a fence covered with graffiti. Notes are written in the margins and between lines of other notes. Scratch-outs appear here and there. Sometimes words are underlined, or sentences have asterisks beside them. It looks as though the notes were written by someone from outer space or, at the very least, in a foreign language.

It's almost always helpful to step back from your reporting and organize your notebook, along with your thoughts as soon after an interview or event as possible, while details are fresh in your mind. Use your notebook to put details into, and use your mind to put the story into perspective.

The End is Near – Almost

So, you've finished your research, and you've got all this stuff piled high. Now what?

Assumedly you have organized your notes in the course of your research, putting apples in one pile, oranges in another and pears in another. Still, you'll usually find you have too much information. This is a plus.

One way to discern what's important is to start writing without looking at your notes. Write from memory. Do a fast draft. What's most important will pop into your mind. Then go back to your research notes and get the exact date, the exact quote or whatever. As you are browsing, you may also stumble across some additional facts you had forgotten about. If you were covering an event, did you get reaction from as broad a spectrum as possible? Their insights add to the perspective in ways you may not have anticipated.

When you are taking photographs, you often take several close-ups, then adjust your lens to get a broader view. Same with reporting. You want to understand and make sense out of the pieces of the puzzle, then you want to draw back and figure where they all fit.

How do you know when you've finished your reporting?

Well, after you've collected enough information to support your story, you should take two more steps:

1. Test the old formula sometimes known as the "5 W's and an H." The letters stood for: Who? What? When? Where? Why? And How? If you can't answer one of those questions, you undoubtedly need to do more reporting.
2. Put yourself in the place of the reader. What questions – large or small – would you want to find out in the story?

If you can answer those questions, then the fun is about to begin: It's time to write.

CHAPTER NINE

How to Write

"My task ... is, by the power of the written word,
to make you hear, to make you feel – it is,
before all, to make you see."

Joseph Conrad

DON MURRAY HAD to walk from one end of the Boston Globe newsroom to the other to get to the Editor's office. The Globe had just hired him as Writing Coach, and this was his first time in the building.

"I know who three of your best writers are," he said. Pointing into the city room, he singled out two women and a man. One of the three was Pulitzer-Prize winning columnist Ellen Goodman whom Murray didn't know by sight at the time.

"OK," I said, "you're right. They are three of the very best. But how did you know?"

"Because," said Murray, "their lips move when they write."

Hundreds of books have been written on the craft of writing, many of the best by Murray. Sitting in on his seminars, reading his books and columns or chatting over lunch, I learned more from Murray than from any of the fine teachers and mentors I have encountered through my career. (Indeed, his byline probably should be on this chapter).

For me to recast the writing lessons from the books piled high in my office would be a disservice. Better you read the real stuff: "The Elements of Style" by William Strunk Jr. and E.B. White; "On Writing Well" by William Zinsser; "Bird by Bird" by Anne Lamott, "The Writing Life" by Annie Dillard, etc.

What I would like to convey here are some of my reflections on writing based on the experience of working in community groups with teens and adults who had little or no writing background.

Beginning, Middle, End

Once the community journalist has completed the research and reporting, the inclination is to plunge into the writing. Arduous reporting creates an impatience to start writing. The impulse should be resisted.

The story should be planned out first, preferably on paper or on the screen. Do an outline, not a formal one with Roman numerals and all, but an outline that organizes the presentation of the material.

Using SilverStringers' software, McGraw-Hill in 2002 developed an exercise as a supplement to its elementary-school textbooks that was quite effective. Called eJournal, the teaching program had three parts, and each part had three steps.

Part One was research. On the screen the pupils were given three questions to answer. Below each question was a box into which they could type their research notes in answer to the questions.

Part Two was organization. Again the screen showed three empty boxes. The students were to organize their three sets of research notes into sentences and paragraphs, eliminating information from notes that lacked importance or relevance.

Part Three was writing. The pupils were to write a report on the subject they had researched. Again they were presented with three boxes, but in this case the boxes would be used to write the beginning, middle and end of their report.

Stories for websites also have a beginning, middle and end that should be reflected in the outline. Spending a lot of time on an elaborate outline will inhibit your writing. Make it a skeleton that you will flesh out in the writing, hopefully with blood rushing through its veins.

Most books on writing have a chapter called Getting Started, which is the biggest stumbling block for new writers. Usually the inability to start a story is a psychological block caused by lack of confidence.

Don Murray at tutoring visit with Melrose SilverStringers.

"If I do not know where to start," wrote Murray, "I find I usually begin with description, writing with information not language, looking at the subject and describing it in revealing details that resonate with the reader."

At another time he wrote, "My columns usually begin with the ordinary. My eye catches a glint from an insignificant element in my life or the lives of those around me and I see it suddenly with humor, anger, sadness, amusement, nostalgia, concern – emotion gives it significance."

Murray has another technique that works well. It's called "The Line". Before getting started, Murray would rapidly write out a series of sentences or phrases that zero in on the point of the story. One line triggers another, sometimes working off the same word or phrase of an earlier line. They're almost like snippets of a headline. He'd dash off 20 or 30 of them before arriving at one that would be "spot on".

Sometimes The Line appears as the start of a story or the third paragraph or maybe even the ending. But it reflects the essence of the story's message

Interestingly, William Faulkner is said to have written his lengthy novels with a 4 x 6 card propped above his typewriter with a few words that described the theme of his story.

Good writers keep a central theme in front of them, either literally or figuratively.

Lots of techniques are used for getting started. Some might even be called gimmicks. Jim was a bright reporter. One day he went to his editor in exasperation.

He had completed several days of reporting an important story and said, "I've been working for 3 hours on writing this story, and I just don't know how to start it." It was suggested he leave off the first paragraph, write the story from the second paragraph to the end, then go back to the editor to discuss what the first paragraph might say.

He did as suggested, but the appropriate first paragraph popped into his mind halfway through writing the story, and he never had to have the conversation with his editor. The start of the story often resides in our subconscious somewhere, and by unfolding the story the appropriate beginning seems to tumble out.

Writing While Standing

Another approach is to just write something – the first thing that comes into your mind. Then go back and redo it when inspiration strikes you. The less you think about it the more likely you'll have a brainstorm. One magazine writer once said she got her "ledes" when she was cooking. "Ledes" is lingo for "leads", meaning the beginning of a story.

Saint-Pol Roux, the surrealist, used to hang a sign on his door when he was sleeping that said, "The Poet is working."

Sportswriters are experts at writing "ledes". Most sports events are at night, so sportswriters often have to write under harsh deadlines. Many will write what is called "running" as a game is in progress. In other words, they actually will be typing the chronological high points of what's going on while the game is in progress. As soon as it's over, they write a first paragraph or two on top of the "running", and a story is immediately ready for the first edition. Since most newspapers have more than one edition, sportswriters write an improved story – often with quotes from the participants and coaches – for the subsequent edition.

At age 18 I covered sports for United Press, mostly professional and college basketball and hockey. The press box was in the middle of the first balcony, and I could easily look down and to my right to see how the Associated Press writer was doing at the end of the game. The name of our game was "Who's first?" There was no time to get hung up on how to start a story.

The easiest way is to begin is with someone's quote, but frankly that can become a lazy device. Still, despite some editors who rule out ever using a "quote lede", they have a time and place.

The Wall Street Journal used to be famous for the case-study approach:

Jeff is going to Singapore next week.

Sally is going to Alaska.

Katy is going to Japan.

It's vacation time, and many high school students are traveling around the world."

The first three examples are simplistic, of course. A real story would have more substance, but this illustrates a way to set up a story about a trend: Three specific examples or cases and a fourth paragraph as a summary of what that trend is.

Profile stories – which we could use more of in the most publications – often begin with a description of the person in a characteristic setting. Narratives use a storyteller's approach, unveiling the elements of the story a little at a time.

Old-fashioned journalism taught the 5 W's and an H approach: Who, what, when, why, where and how. "The Senate voted today to provide funding for fuel assistance." It's still a good approach for certain basic news stories in an online publication, but most often it is reserved for two or three-paragraph stories.

Good to the Last Drop

Don't worry about which type of opening you use. Let the story dictate that. Novelist Gabriel Garcia Marquez summed up the importance of a first paragraph when he said this about it: "The theme is defined, the style, the tone."

Interestingly, few writing books devote a chapter to endings. How unfortunate. The last paragraph may be final, but it also lingers in the reader's mind. Make a special effort with the closing.

It should not be a summary. In some way the ending should capture the essence of the story. It may be a nugget of information that you have stored up like a squirrel. Many good writers often know what they are going to say in the last paragraph before they write the first paragraph. The possibilities are endless (pun intended). Look at how other good writers end their stories to get some ideas.

The beginning and the ending should echo one another, holding together the middle, as though they were two pieces of bread in a sandwich. Speaking of food, do you often leave the last good bite of a meal till the end? Readers of stories also like to savor that last bite of information.

The Thrill of Discovery

Consumers had become so accustomed to having stories delivered to them on a platter by the media that they have forgotten the nuances of storytelling, a practice that dates back to the beginning of time.

Think of writing as a conversation. If you read James Nuland's book, *How to Die?*, you would have seen a quote from Laurence Stone, an 18th-Century novelist: "Writing is but a different name for conversation." Or as Don Murray would say, "Their lips move when they write."

Writing is a personal process, so maybe it's appropriate that the three main elements Murray has identified in stories all start with the letter "I". They are:

1. **Information** – words are symbols for what we learn.
2. **Importance** – that is, what is significant (which we often find in the insignificant details).
3. **Interest** – if it affects the reader, it has passed the test.

Think of writing as discovery. Let yourself go and be surprised about what happens. Walt Whitman once said he never knew how his poems would end: "I just let her come until the fountain is dry." Edward Albee is quoted as having said, "I write to find out what I'm thinking about."

Some people find they can write better without using notes, then come back and fill in the details. Don't worry about spelling or punctuation or capitalization or grammar. Faulkner said, "There are some kinds of writing that you have to do very fast, like riding a bicycle on a tightrope."

Think of writing as art. You are an artist and a sculptor. You are unfolding patterns of information that have meaning, that the reader needs to see. Give them context: "The town's first bowling alley was located above Maguire's Drugstore, virtually in the center of downtown." Or: "The Fletchers are a well-known family in Hudson. Bob and his brother, Ed, were outstanding athletes. Their father ran the city's major furniture company. Their uncle was mayor for many years."

Now you become the sculptor. You're fashioning a sculpture in writing – molding, shaping, adding, subtracting . . . The first draft is when you take a big chunk of clay and sort of mold it into a shape that looks roughly like a bust of a person. You have a *rough* idea that this glob of clay has a chin and a nose . . . but the eyes and lips are not apparent. You are writing a *rough* draft. You discover as you write.

On Being Authoritative

It's important to write with authority, because written words carry weight. How can you be sure to do so?

The techniques vary slightly based on the type of writing you are doing. Let's confine our attention to *opinion writing* and *news/feature writing*.

On opinion: A person can write with authority if he or she is a bona fide expert on a subject. Otherwise, it is necessary to quote others, in effect borrowing the expertise of others. It also lends authority to include the arguments of those who take the opposite position from yours.

On news/feature: Writing style is one way of instilling authority, but a surefire way is to do extensive reporting. We differentiate for the reader between material that we know through our own accord with what we obtain from other sources. Two basic types fall under the "know-of-your-own-accord" category: common knowledge and what we see/hear ourselves. It is common knowledge, for instance, that Pearl Harbor was attacked on December 7, 1941, so we don't have to credit the Pentagon for that fact. If we attend a soccer game and see the player score by kicking a high shot with his right foot, we don't have to quote the coach to that effect. Otherwise we employ attribution both to provide verification and to instill authority. The most common form of attribution is linking a person or written source to a direct or indirect quote. However, any proprietary information that is obtained through reporting or research should be attributed – and that includes public information. It is important to weave attribution into the story as elegantly as possible so that the story doesn't read like a bumpy road. In some cases, when information from several sources is intermingled in a story, it is appropriate to carry a line at the end of the story, possibly in italics or in parentheses, giving credit: (Some information from this story came from Associated Press reports and from the Encyclopedia Britannica). This often occurs when historical information is incorporated into the story. The use of confidential or unnamed sources should be avoided altogether. In the professional press there are times this practice is appropriate. However, even in those cases, strict adherence to certain procedures must be carried out to maintain integrity and even at times withstand legal action.

Web Writing

Why in the world would you write differently for the Web than you would for a print publication? Simple: The readers' mindset is different. When readers go on the internet, they tend to have clickitis, jumping from one place to another. Generally speaking, therefore, stories should be short. But now always by any means.

Finding a strong, single theme works for photos too as winter draws near an end with rose hips peeking through the snow cap. (Photo by Jim Cerny)

A lot of the attributes of a story written for print apply online as well: The story should have a single, dominant theme; it should be timely and relevant. Stories with photographs attract higher readership, we have learned from studies through the years, but so far it's unclear whether Web stories with imbedded video or audio attract or distract. Links have the advantage of supplementing a story, but they too can send the reader away, never to return to your story.

Still, it behooves Web writers to emulate radio writing by sticking with shorter, punchier sentences, by using strong verbs and crisp adjectives (sparingly), by writing conversationally or with an attitude when appropriate and by employing techniques such as breaking out items with numbers or bullets or integrating graphical elements into the type.

These devices are especially helpful when writing long stories, which definitely have a place on the Web. For the most part, however, you should go to great lengths to keep your stories short.

On Being a Revisionist

> *"I love revision. Where else can spilled milk be turned into ice cream?"*
> *– Author Katherine Patterson*

What does it mean to revise? Breaking the verb into its parts, it means "to see again?" It does not mean editing. Editing is getting a story ready for the reader; revising is the luxury of satisfying yourself as the writer. You should wallow in it.

Think of revision as an ongoing process that starts when you first think about how you will write a story to the point when you turn it over to an editor. Think of it as being nothing but a fun, positive process.

Revision *is* writing. Writing Coach Murray has written a whole book on the topic of revision. He says, "Rewriting begins before you put the first word on paper and continues until you edit the final draft – which may, in turn, inspire revision." He taught that the three secrets to good writing are: (1) revise; (2) revise, and (3) revise.

Reporters driving back to the newspaper after an assignment, run ideas through their minds of various versions for the "line" or the opening sentence or the closing sentence.

Then when they get back to the office, they pour it out as fast as the mind can recreate it, changing it as they went along, not worrying about spelling or capitalization or punctuation, just getting words on paper. Then they might walk to the water cooler.

Returning to the key board, they either tear up what they had done and start over with a totally new fast draft or begin revising. The revision process: How does that work? First you give your story a quick scan for obvious additions or deletions, still not worried about grammar or such fine points.

Then read it aloud to yourself. Now that sounds contradictory, but try it, and you will discover that you can actually hear the music of your writing. Sometimes it sounds pretty nice. Other times you choke on a discordant note.

After that, go through the piece from top to bottom, asking yourself a variety of questions that soon became second nature:

Is it accurate? When in doubt, check it out. When I would ask my father how to spell a word, he would always respond the same way: "Look it up." The same is true with facts. Don't guess. Don't rely on someone else. Check them out.

Is it focused? By that it is meant, is there a single theme throughout. If you have written a "line", is every sentence supportive of it. If not, the sentence will be distracting to the reader and should be eliminated. At this point, try writing a title for the piece. Not a headline, but a title. You'd be surprised how that helps clarify the focus.

Is it too long or too short? Once I wrote a piece for an MIT publication based on an interview of more than an hour. I was told to keep the story to 300 words. That's not much. Then I was told it would be the cover piece of this issue and therefore could only be 200 words long. My second piece was better than the first.

Is the story clear? An editor I once worked for used to say, "The readers you care about live in three deckers, not in the ivory tower at Harvard."

Are things in the right order? Some people actually try writing an outline *after* they write their story.

Does it flow? Kurt Vonnegut, the novelist, says, "Don't put anything in a story that does not reveal the character or advance the action." The same is true for the kinds of stories you write for your online publication.

Is there enough significant detail? Is there enough or too much description?

Is it the right "voice" for the story? You don't write an obituary with a flippant tone.

Is it me? Only you can answer that question, but after a while you will see that you have developed a style of writing, just as you have a style for carrying on conversations, whether you realize it or not.

Then there are two bigger questions?

Where is the tension in the story? The rain fell for 36 hours. So what? The rain fell for 36 hours and forced 300 people out of their homes in Helsinki.

Does the story contain any surprise(s). When you learn from the reporting process – or even the writing process – then what surprised you will most likely surprise the reader – or most of them anyway. "In 1956 Helsinki experienced its worst flooding. The Fire Department had to pump out 50 basements of homes. This week the Fire Department pumped out 250 basements. In '56, 10 roads had to be closed. This week 25 roads were closed to automobiles . . . etc."

Now that you have answered all these questions, you can go back and fix up your typing and the grammar and take out all the cliches and jargon!

Remember, revision is the fun part of writing. Or as Bernard Malamud used to say, "I love the flowers of afterthought."

Good writers spend lots of time at revision. Don't be fooled by how simple and clear some of their writing seems to be. The late Harvard economist/author John Kenneth Galbraith once wrote:

"In my own case there are days when the result is so bad that no fewer than five revisions are required. However, when I'm greatly inspired, only four revisions are needed before, as I've often said, I put in that note of spontaneity which even my meanest critics concede."

CHAPTER TEN

How to Edit

*"Editors should be more like
intellectual bartenders
than chefs"*

Esther Dyson

EDITING, DONE WELL, is an unselfish act. The image of the wide-eyed, salivating editor wielding an ax is passé.

Indeed, editors at their best are the ambassadors of ideas and the finished carpenters of words.

Community journalism heightens the concept that everyone involved in a publication can and should be an editor as seen in its broadest context.

The definition of editing goes beyond the critical function of fixing up spelling and punctuation. It is a continuum that starts with the germ of an idea and never ceases even after publication.

Group Editing

Practitioners of community journalism catch on quickly to the team concept. While they may not be under the same daily or even hourly pressure of a professional, they still are pressed for time, going to school, working or even keeping up with the not-so-laid-back lifestyle of today's retirees.

The seed of a story idea is planted among the group members, usually sitting around a table or communicating through email, by the person who pursues the story or by someone else in the group who for one reason or other is not doing the story.

Frequently a community journalist will say something like, "I'm working on two stories right now, but there is a meeting tomorrow night that should produce a good story . . ."

Except when planning a major project or coverage of a big story, sharing by reporters around a table doesn't happen too often among professionals, nor does the next step when members of the group start suggesting ways to make it a better story: people worth interviewing, where to get information, what might make a good accompanying photo, etc. This is editing, the unselfish shaping of an idea for someone else to work on.

Pre-Story Editing

Stepping back, editing should flow from the group's mission. A community site probably wouldn't feel the need for a story on the anatomy of a fruit fly. That would hardly fit in with a mission that calls for stories that are be about or of particular interest to residents of a particular community. However, a story on what causes fruit flies and how to deal with them might be particularly relevant, especially in warm climes.

When someone comes to a meeting with eyes lighted up and says, "I've got this great idea for a story . . .", it usually works out. However, there are those who have the germ of an idea but can't quite articulate it ("I'm wrestling with . . .). This is the point at which others become ambassadors of ideas. Through prompting, nudging, cajoling, or maybe some slight pushing, they delicately and diplomatically help draw out the idea.

A woman sheepishly suggested she might do a story on the local garden club, because volunteers had helped beautify one of the major traffic circles in town. Soon, from among the dozen attendees, came mention of six other projects the garden club had taken on, and the idea for a broader, more substantive story began to take shape.

Occasionally a person will join a community journalism group and not have the foggiest idea what to write. Some newcomers sit through several meetings without writing anything, before someone has the presence of mind to ask: What interests you? What intrigues you? What are you curious about? What's hot in your neighborhood – what issue, what trend, what upcoming event?

Getting over that first-story hurdle can be difficult, and, like learning to ride a bike, might need a helper. But once up and pedaling, the knack quickly becomes almost second nature.

The Conversation

As stated previously, writing is conversation, and the early sounding out is best done with an editor. The writer speaks; the editor listens. Sometimes the story takes shape in the writer's mind during that conversation without the editor even responding. Good listening can be the best form of editing, be it online or by telephone or in person.

Conversation should be taking place not only when the idea is first being formulated; but during and after the reporting phase; it should take place before the story is written, and it should take place after an editor has fully processed the story. "The Editor" is your community group. Some of this conversation can be pretty brief ("This week I talked with . . . and, and this is what I found out . . .").

At each stage the editor should bear in mind that it is the reporter's story on the one hand, but it also is the reader's story. It is not the editors' story. Thus the editing should generally take the form of questions readers might ask when they come to the story cold (How was he dressed? When did she say that? Where did it occur?). When editors start dictating what should go into a story, they tend to stifle the conversation and the story. On the other hand, editors should speak up if there are gaps in the story; that is, elements that make the story incomplete. And they should speak up when a story is too long, unclear, awkward, meandering, etc. It's a bit like pulling a wagon: The job is easier when two people are pulling, rather than one, especially when the two are pulling together.

Improving vs. Ruining

Try comparing the development of a story to baking a loaf of bread. All of the elements need to be brought together and kneaded. Then the dough is popped into the oven until it rises and is ready to eat.

Editors and reporters should be collaborators in the development of story ideas. It shouldn't matter who has the initial idea. What matters is how the idea is molded and framed into a better idea.

Let's say someone wants to do a story on how to make bread. The editor might suggest providing some historical perspective, pointing out that before the 20th Century B.C. there was evidence Egyptians baked bread as did the Swiss Lake Dwellers in the early days of civilized Europe.

That might prompt the writer to recall religious connotations to bread: manna from heaven to feed the Israelites; Jesus calling himself "the bread of life" and the ritual of bread and wine being served in Christian traditions.

Soon a simple four-paragraph story can become a story with substance. Part of this illustration is based on the evolution of an actual story.

The point is that we shouldn't be satisfied with the first idea that comes to mind. That's only the beginning. We should turn it over in our minds, shape it, pull it apart, push it back together again. You know, like kneading.

Now, some editors might say you can't write a story about bread without referring to peanut butter! And you, of course, might be inclined to say that's a half-baked idea. In all seriousness, an editor can ruin a good story by imposing too many elements. A small suggestion here and there is fine, but generally the story should contain what the writer deems most relevant and is most comfortable with. It is the writer's story.

Finding Holes

On the other hand, an editor or just someone in your group whom you regularly turn to for an informal reading of your story before it is submitted, can often be like a detective, finding holes in the story that need filling. A writer can get too close to a story and leave out a crucial detail or assume the reader knows certain information.

It is at this stage that, when a story is turned in, an editor needs to be the alter ego for the reader, anticipating what the reader is likely to know or not know. A fair story can sometimes be made into a good one fairly easily.

Continuing to bear in mind that it is the writer's story (a deliberate repetition), an editor should approach the final draft in the following manner:

- Errors in spelling and punctuation should be fixed.
- Deletion of a few words here and there that will tighten up the story should be handled without hesitation.
- Major changes or insertions of material should occur only in collaboration with the writer.

On the one hand, no story should be published without it going through an editor. On the other hand, no story requiring lots of editing changes should be published without the writer's knowledge or consent. It's a team effort. What's the definition of "major changes"? Clearly that's a judgment call, but the easiest way to make the determination is for the editor to put himself or herself in the shoes of the writer: "Would I want to know about or have a say in these changes?"

Good writers know it's smart to turn in their stories early, rather than right on deadline. Editors under deadline sometimes have to make changes without the writer's knowledge. Good writers also know that editors can improve the way a story reads or ask appropriate questions they think would be raised in the mind of the reader. There's no such thing as a bad question.

However, there is such a thing as bad editing. That's what occurs when an editor plunges ahead with changes that cross the line from editing into rewriting. The most effective editing tool is a little conversation or an exchange of email. In the end the editing goal is to make the writer's story good enough to become the reader's story.

Looking Before Leaping

The final polishing of a story is called copy editing. The roles of story editing and copy editing can be rolled into one person, but even in community publications with small staffs it's preferable to divide the functions. Copy editing not only is a last check on the writer but also is an insurance check on the work of the story editor.

My advice to a copy editor who receives a story is to put down your pencil if the story is on paper or put down the mouse for a computer-generated story. Give the story a quick read from top to bottom, not worrying about details but getting a feel for the essence of the story.

This quick step, whether the story is short or long, conditions the mind for the fine-tuning work that is ahead. Instructors in speed writing emphasize a similar approach to reading a book: Look over the front and back flaps of the cover, skim the table of contents, flip through the pages getting a sense of the type size, frequently mentioned names and the rough length of chapters. It's like pressing down on your pillow to put the dent in the right place before putting your head into it.

The quick scan often is the best time to figure out what's not in a story as opposed to what's in the story. In looking at the big picture are there missing elements that are essential to the point of the story? Missing elements are often referred to as "holes", for obvious reasons.

An easy example would be a something like: "The teacher made three points." And then the story only lists two.

What comes out of a story to make it better is easier to determine than what should be there but isn't. Usually, these holes become obvious if the editor puts herself or himself in the role of the reader. The question is: Does this story answer all the questions that would pop into a reader's mind? Bear in mind that all readers are not necessarily acquainted with the subject matter of the story.

If a story says a rock band is the second most popular, what is the first? If it says her background makes her qualified for the position, what is her background? If it quotes a liberal on a controversial issue, what is the conservative position? What is the moderate position? Are there other positions on the same issue (don't fall into the trap of thinking there are only two sides to every issue)?

The trick is to keep stories as compact and complete as possible.

Think of stories as a whole and make sure there are no holes.

Accomplished copy editors are equipped with alarm bells in their heads. A misspelling, wrong choice of word, poor grammar or misused punctuation sets off the alarm. The alarm is less annoying, more useful and more accurate than automatic spell check or grammar check.

The copy editor will go into mull mode when coming across a word with an "ei" in the middle, subconsciously reciting, "I before E, except after C . . . etc." Certain words will set set lights flashing, such as "median", which often is used as a synonym for "average", which it ain't.

When in Doubt, Leave It Out

Punctuation? It has a function. It is often overused.

If you are in a foreign country, you have difficulty getting around without signs. More and more signs are minimizing the use of words and using symbols, because not everyone speaks the native language. So when you are driving and you see a sign with an arrow bending to the right, you know there's a curve ahead. Sometimes you may have to look twice to distinguish between the signs for the ladies' room and the men's room, but obviously these symbols are useful guides.

The same is true with punctuation. Its function is to help guide the reader through the sentence or paragraph in a way that will make the wording more understandable. Many books have been written about the rules of punctuation, but in less than a minute consider these points about commas:

* Commas do not signal a pause, so don't drop them into a sentence without a reason.

EXAMPLE: The girl went to the store and bought milk (no comma, because "went" and "bought: have the same subject: "girl"). However, the girl went to the store, and the boy went to school (has a comma, because it is as though two sentences are joined by an "and").

In a series you have a choice as to whether to use two or three commas.

EXAMPLE: She liked vanilla, chocolate, strawberry and chocolate chip. Newspapers usually omit the comma after "strawberry", because years ago type was set by hand, so they tried to avoid punctuation marks whenever possible.

Most publications have stylebooks to provide consistency when usage and punctuation rules have variables, such as in the last example. The stylebook came into vogue, because there are so many variations. Most publications lean on the Associated Press stylebook, but the Times of London has a good, quick online reference among others. What's important is that everyone uses the same stylebook. The same goes for use of a dictionary. Webster, for instance, has a variety of editions within which there are occasional differences in word spellings. Lacking a stylebook, a community journalist simply should use common sense and think twice before typing a comma or other punctuation mark into a sentence. When in doubt, leave it out.

Why is punctuation important? Because it can tell you whether a question is being asked or a statement is being made. A comma can introduce a list. A dash can emphasize an interruption or change in tone. A semicolon may be used to link closely related independent clauses (which otherwise could stand alone as a sentence). Parentheses can set off relevant but not necessarily vital information. Usually grammar books carry a chapter just on commas

If you are tempted to use a comma after a phrase at the beginning of a sentence, ask yourself if the phrase would call for commas were it placed elsewhere in the sentence. For instance:

In the event of rain, the game will be postponed.
The game will be postponed in the event of rain.
The first example should lose the comma.

Sloppiness Starts With Start

These examples are shorter than an editor normally encounters, but, when the editor is unsure of whether a sentence needs a comma, he or she can strip away a lot of the verbiage and boil the problem down to the essentials – subjects and verbs – to make a determination.

So, you say, what's the big deal? An extra comma here, a missing comma there?

There are two ways of looking at it. Commas and other punctuation are helpful road signs for readers. When misused or used inconsistently, they are a sign of sloppiness to the reader.

A final note on sloppiness. Sometimes stories are turned over to the copy editors with crazy spacing, obvious typing errors, capitals where lower case is obviously called for, etc. Professionals and community journalists are both guilty of this practice. It can become a lazy habit, like leaving clothes on the bedroom floor. A writer who persists in submitting sloppy copy should have the story sent back. The copy editor's job should never entail cleaning up after the writer.

Headlines & Captions

The copy editor still has vital functions to complete after fine-tuning a story. Next come the embellishments.

The written matter of a story often is referred to as "the body". What goes on a body? You got it on the first try: A head. Now you are fluent in journalese, because a "head" or "hed" is the coined word for headline.

Headlines differ from titles. They are more like sentences with article adjectives left out to save space and enable quick reading by the browser.

Titles go on books and poems and generally are more like labels. They occasionally have a use on a column or a feature. Headlines tend to have active verbs. They have two basic duties:

1.   To reflect the essentials of the story.
2.   To draw the reader into the story.

Headlines often – but not always – summarize the story. They always should be consistent with the tone of the story. And they occasionally may titillate.

Extreme care needs to be taken with the writing of a headline. It speaks to the reader and says: "This is worth reading, because . . .". Otherwise the reader moves on. It doesn't matter how well reported or how well written a story is if the headline does not convey the sense of the story and entice the reader to take a looksee. A headline is like a greeting: It can be welcoming or off-putting.

That's why good editors will try numerous drafts of headlines on a story before arriving at one that is satisfactory. The selection of nouns, verbs, adjectives and adverbs is especially important. Choosing just the right word can illuminate.

A headline in smaller type under the main headline is often called a subhed. Its purpose usually is to expand on the idea in the top headline or to interject a second thought. Generally the main hed expresses a single thought or point.

Finally there is an animal called the crosshead. Placed intermittently throughout the text of a story crossheads have a couple of purposes: to break up masses of type; to indicate change of subject. Usually their type size is only slightly larger than that of the story, and the type is in bold or in a headline font. They can be written with or without verbs.

The ultimate responsibility for a headline resides with the editor. However, community writers should be encouraged to put headlines on their stories before turning them in, because the writers have the best feel for their stories and have a stake in what should be stressed. Editors, on the other hand, may write a new hed, because they are less attached to the story and more conversant with the role of the headline as it pertains to reflecting the essentials and tone of the story while at the same time being a magnet for readership.

Every reader survey we had done at the Boston Globe – and we did a lot of them from the late sixties to the early nineties – reflected a significant increase in readership for stories that were accompanied by at least one photograph or one piece of art (sketch, map, graphic). Part of the editor responsibility is to think visually. Since space is not an issue on the Web as it is in a newspaper or magazine, photos and artwork should accompany virtually every story.

Just as a headline can sell a story, so too can a caption sell a photo. Eye tracking studies show a rapid moving back and forth between the photo and the caption, generally written by an editor. The problem with most captions is that they say too much. The picture tells a story in and of itself. The purpose of the caption is not to retell the story told by the photo but to enhance the visual story. And if the photo accompanies a story – which most often is the case – the caption doesn't need a lot of verbiage.

*Few words are needed in captions for photos such as this one of row boat in
early morning (Photo by Jim Cerny)*

Occasionally there is call for a story-in-caption photo. This is a photo that doesn't have a story connected to it, so the role of the caption is to be expansive and in effect be a story.

In its November, 2005, edition the Melrose Mirror carried a stunning picture by Don Norris of the local school in the process of being torn down, and in an unusual twist the caption was written in the first person:

NOSTALGIA: The date is October 23, 2005. The picture is the current condition of Melrose High School, ca1932, taken from the top of the football stands. On the top floor I can see the lab where Harold Poole taught chemistry, Mr. Boyle taught botany, and the classroom where Miss Amy Damon taught English. On the second floor I can make out the room where Miss Alice Heald taught French and Mr. Warren Nash introduced us to Russian. At the right is all that remains of Doc Clark's original gymnasium, and below that, the woodworking shop and classrooms of Coach Dave Gavin and Stan Battles. We have no story on the demise of the old building for this issue, but we do have several other linked photos showing the "progress" of demolition. Just click on the big picture.

When Rye Reflections began publishing, it carried a bright red photo at the top of the front page showing the sun rising over the harbor. The photo and caption were used as a story package to introduce the new publication and some of the contents of the maiden issue. Here is the how the caption was worded:

WITH DAWN'S RISING OVER RYE HARBOR comes a new citizen venture. Find out more about this publication and its creators in the WHO WE ARE section. Read about Mimi White's laurels while enjoying work by local writers in the POETRY section. Meditate on the meaning of Memorial Day in the OPINION section. Explore the photos and stories throughout; give us your feedback; likes, dislikes, and suggestions as Rye Reflections attempts to mirror the interests of those who experience that special feeling at sunrise and sunset.

Style questions arise in practically every segment of a website. Some are less important than others, especially in the early going when there are more pressing needs. But captions are highly visible. Should the type be roman or italic? What size type and what font? Should one-line captions be centered or flush left? Should all-cap lead-in words be used for captions that run more than one-line long? What about the placement, type size, font and wording of the photo credit?

Perhaps someone should do an exhaustive study to find out how credits are handled and what's the most popular placement. Some are flush right between the photo and the caption, some are under the caption, and some are placed sideways along the outer edge of the photo.

Few may agree with me, but I think all of those approaches do an injustice to the photographer. The credit is generally in small type and it appears to be floating. Placing a credit under the photo also separates the caption, albeit a short distance, but it breaks up what I see as a package. To me the package should contain photo, caption and credit. My recommendation on the placement is to put the photographer's name in parenthesis at the end of the caption and in the same type size and font as the rest of the caption. It's easier on the reader, better for the photographer and eliminates one more line of code that needs to be written.

Still, I'm comfortable with all the other approaches, providing you don't find one style on one page and another elsewhere.

Cat-in-the-Hat Editing

In summation, the community journalist wears many editing hats. To punctuate this point I once came up with an at-a-glance list, admittedly stretched:

As missionary

Does the story idea fit the mission of the publication? *The writer should maintain a sense of individuality within the framework of the group.*

As ambassador

What diplomatic approach best stimulates good story ideas? *For new members in particular, what interests her or him? What issue is the writer passionate about? What intrigues them? What are they curious about? What's "hot" where they live (event, trend or issue)? With a little prodding, cajoling, questioning, how can the story idea be improved?*

As listener

Who goes first? Why? *It's the writer's story from start to finish.*

Assume the role of responder. *Let the writer explain his or her concept of the story in mind. Then have a conversation about it.*

Continually raise the question: What would the reader ask? *Ultimately the reader is the customer, and the customer knows best.*

As baker

When is kneading needed? *Resume the conversation after the writer has done some reporting.*

When does the recipe need supplementing? *Does it contain perspective through references to history or comparison or varying points of view?*

As salad mixer

What good is a salad without dressing? What is most needed to supplement the story? *Headlines, photos & captions, art, map, links …*

What is the role of salad dressing? *Bring out taste; supplement or embellish it; reflect essence of story (you don't put oil and vinegar on a Caesar Salad). Make it more attracting to reader)*

As grammarian

Why do grammar and punctuation matter? *Signs clarify.*

Why is the role of the editor is like that of a barber or hairdresser? *Clip, don't butcher; shape, don't realign; fulfill will of customer.*

As Sherlock Holmes

Does every word count? *At 15 cents for each unnecessary word I find, how much could I earn from your story?**

What's lacking? *Find what's not in the story: Are all questions answered; all sides reflected?*

(* In my college years I was one of four junior rewrite reporters on the night shift in the Boston Globe sports department. Each of us would write 15 to 30 stories a night of varying lengths. They'd range in length between 100 and 1000 words. The stories were written on typewriters in that era, and we all kept carbon copies of our stories.

(At the end of the night, when the early edition had been published and most normal people were sleeping, it would quiet down. At that point we would trade our carbon copies, and each reporter would review the others' stories to see what words could be cut out without hurting the story. For every word that could be cut out, we had to pay our colleague 10 cents.

(Soon we all became what is often called "tight writers". We also became pretty good editors. Try trading stories with a friend via email before sending the stories to your editor and see who can delete the most unessential words. You may not get rich, but it's a fun way to think more carefully about writing tightly.)

Here's another exercise: Go back over the above four paragraphs and see how many words can be deleted without hurting the message. I estimate there are about 15. At the rate of 15 cents a word (inflation, you know) that's $1.50 I owe you.

One Last Step

The editor's role doesn't end after all these steps are completed, from story editing through to copy editing. After all is said and done, there is one more step. If there is time, it's a good idea to walk away from the story and do something else for a while. That last step? Re-read the story.

After all that, it may not be perfect, but it's the best you can do. You can now take your hat off to yourself.

CHAPTER ELEVEN

What We've Learned

*"Wherever you are – if you are following
your bliss, you are enjoying the refreshment, that
life within you . . ."*

Joseph Campbell, "The Power of Myth"

WHAT HAVE WE learned and what does the future of group journalism hold?

We have learned that: Anyone can be a productive part of a citizen-journalism group, and some can experience dramatic achievements.

"Somehow we became convinced that only a few special people have talents or visions worth pursuing. But that moment is ending," MIT professor Henry Jenkins was quoted as observing in J.D. Lasica's book, "Darknet."

Though not called a citizen journalist at the time (1958), Ty Abate was proof of the concept that journalism is learnable.

The father of eight children and a father figure to hundreds of others, Abate worked in a factory and coached Little League baseball for many years in Haverhill, Mass. Even when players graduated from high school or college, Abate (pronounced A-bah-tee) kept in close touch.

When an entrenched daily newspaper, *the Haverhill Gazette*, was hit by a strike, a new newspaper, called *the Haverhill Journal,* started up with the support of union and non-union laborers, twenty of whom volunteered their time to help.

Abate would show up in the newspaper office every day after work and lend his sports expertise to the Sports Editor, yours truly.

Abate, age 34, was not much more than 5 feet tall, a quiet man, always neatly dressed and always wearing a Red Sox baseball cap with the long, curled visor casting a constant shadow over his thin, brown face. I found him to be more valuable than a library.

After a couple of weeks, I said, "Ty, why don't you write a sports column for us? Everyone in town knows you and you know more about Haverhill sports than anyone."

At that point he sheepishly informed me that he had only a sixth-grade education and couldn't write. So I suggested he come in the next day with an idea for a column and some notes, and I would be his private ghostwriter. This routine went on for about two weeks, a column appearing every day with his photo at the top, wearing his trademark Red Sox cap. One of the most famous sportswriters in Boston during the 40's and 50's was Dave Egan, who wrote for the Hearst newspaper under the title, "The Colonel". Harvard-educated and hardly known for being a teetotaler, Egan made a reputation for incisive writing that tended to torment the high and mighty, especially Ted Williams.

So we labeled Abate's column, "The Little Colonel". He was too gentle a man to skewer any athlete, but that wasn't what attracted readers. Abate loved sports and the athletes in his community. His column was an instant hit and prompted lots of feedback. Abate had to fight his way down the street to get to our office, because everyone wanted to stop and talk with him.

After a couple of weeks Abate began submitting hand-written drafts of columns that needed a good rewrite. A week or two after that his drafts only needed heavy editing. After a month he had taught himself to write reasonably well and required a minimum of mentoring . . . er, coaching.

Later Abate quit his job at the factory and became a fulltime sports columnist. He had the passion. He cared about young people. He felt compelled to tell their stories. Like some of the athletes he wrote about, all Abate needed was a little encouragement to take on a role he never dreamed he could achieve. He became a star.

A couple of years later he was hired as a sports columnist by the Manchester Union Leader, New Hampshire's statewide newspaper, and was chosen the state's Sportswriter of the Year in 1967. Three years later, at age 48, he died suddenly.

In modern times we have pretty much left formal storytelling to the professionals. What a shame. We all have an innate ability for storytelling. The emergence of the internet is starting to make this clear.

'Diary of a Hobo'

Bill Jodrey was almost 85 years old before he and others learned of his gift for storytelling. Unlike Abate, Jodrey as a young man had contemplated writing a book. It was to be based on his experiences as a hobo. But – at least then – it was not to be. "Nobody will be interested in reading about that," a friend told Jodrey, then in his early 20's. Discouraged, Jodrey put away a notebook he had kept during his journeys and forgot about taking on a book.

Sixty years later he joined an internet publishing group, the Melrose SilverStringers, and revived the dream. Three years later, at age 87, he published a book.

Bill Jodrey, the former hobo, strikes normal pose at SilverStringers meeting.
(Photo by Don Norris)

Jodrey had little to say at the first few meetings he attended. He had the bearing of an erect English country gentleman, although he never graduated from high school. Balding on top, he had white hair, a white mustache and always wore a neat shirt with a string tie and a checkered wool coat sweater. He'd sit at the meeting table with the other members of the group for a couple of hours at a time, barely speaking, his large hands folded in front of him. Even for someone just over 6 feet tall, the size of his hands stood out, strengthened by twenty years of steering a crane.

After a few months Jodrey turned out to be the most prolific writer in the group. His stories – about fifty in five years – were always short, frequently understated but always absorbing. Positive reader reaction poured in, spurring him on.

A lot of Jodrey's stories had to do with his trip across the country and back as a hobo during the Depression when he was 19 years old. After he had written half a dozen stories, I jokingly said to him, "You should write a book."

Three months later he handed me 26 chapters.

He asked me to edit them. I was further dumbfounded when I read his stories. They were fascinating. But they had one major flaw: They were too short. After forty years of dealing with overwriting by most newspaper reporters, this was a new challenge for me. Clearly Jodrey's taciturn personality spilled over into his writing style.

What to do?

Jodrey lived alone in a small apartment in a senior housing complex, his wife having died several years earlier. So, I sat him down at his kitchen table with a tape recorder and started asking him questions to draw out more detail chapter by chapter: What did the town look like? Describe the soup kitchen. What did the first hoboes you met look like? How did they smell? Did they say much? What kind of conversation did you have with the little boy who hopped the train? Did he talk about his parents? Were there women hoboes?

The responses spewed out of him. He had a photographic memory. His notebook, which he still had after 65 years, was virtually irrelevant. Clearly he grasped what was needed to flesh out his stories, so I only had to run through three or four chapters with him. He got the idea.

Three months later he gave me another 26 chapters, totally rewritten. They were still written in his understated way but with more detail. In 2001 "Diary of a Hobo" was published.

'Do You Like Cornbread?'

The stories in Jodrey's book are real. They are not overstated. They are a lens through which a little-told side of the Depression story is related: not from Wall Street, but from the highways and the byways of cities and small towns, from the prairies and the hills, in the diners and at the churches, in private homes, automobiles, trucks and freight cars.

It is an uplifting depiction of a time when compassion was more than a word in a slogan. It is storytelling in the best sense of the tradition, because we learn so much by sharing in what Jodrey saw, heard and felt.

A seventh-grade teacher in Newmarket, N.H., used "Diary of a Hobo" in her two reading classes. She then came up with an exercise to help the students learn how to express themselves. As the result, 50 of them wrote letters to Jodrey, expressing what they liked about the book, specifying what parts had the most impact on them and winding up with questions that were left in their minds.

Here's a sample of their questions:

How did you brush your teeth?
Was it scary? When you get in someone's car that you don't know, who knows what they'll do?
I would like to know if you had other "adventures" with a girl, like the one you had with the car driver ... I want to know if other things happened but you didn't talk about it in your book.

Are you a Patriots' fan?
How could you stand the smell without taking a shower?
How much weight did you lose?
Is your story entirely true?
What was the grossest thing you ate as a hobo?
How do you feel about people's feelings toward strangers now compared to then?
Do you like cornbread?

You can imagine what a thrill it was for Jodrey, then age 89, to receive letters from these inquisitive minds as he sat in his daughter Elaine's living room in Ocala, Florida, where he was recuperating from a series of small strokes. He died there at age 91.

When people of all kinds with various degrees of wisdom come together in community, they are like the tape recorder was to Jodrey. They stimulate the memory, sharpen the focus and enrich the storytelling.

Real-Life Storytelling

A final brief example of the power of storytelling also relates to a SilverStringer, Jini Hanley, now deceased, one of the founding members, who wrote an article on the eve of the anniversary of Pearl Harbor in 1998 entitled, "The War Department regrets . . ." Hanley told how her brother Neil had been killed in World War II, but her other brother, Jim, survived. She wrote:

"When Jim finally came home in May 1946, he was warmly greeted by my mother and me and our dog, Gyp. An hour later, we realized that Gyp had gone outside. He was sitting on the porch looking down the street. He was smart enough to realize that two boys had gone away so two should be coming home. It took us about a week to convince him that Neil was gone for good."

Citizen journalism sites need to provide some of the news of their communities that is not being covered by local newspapers, but the sites also are vehicles for making news more relevant through storytelling.

We have learned that: Face-to-face group meetings produce built-in idea tweaking, a sense of sharing, social and intellectual fulfillment, a support system and the most important benefit: They're fun.

One Melrose woman turned to the Stringers at a weekly meeting for support. Referring to her husband, she said: "He tells me I shouldn't be working at my computer at 1 o'clock in the morning. Doesn't he understand? I'm writing!!"

Everyone chuckled – sympathetically.

The Junior Journal probably would still be publishing were it not for the fact that the editors grew up and went off to college. A couple of attempts to organize renewal meetings, one in Europe and the other at an undetermined locale in the Mediterranean area, fell through due to lack of sponsorship. Plenty of writers were still poised to contribute from around the world, but virtual training of editors proved too difficult.

We have learned that: Unlike blogs, community publications prefer a review process for stories and media. It's a team process. Editing tends to be light and polite, but over time editors tend to be more assertive in a helpful way and writers tend to be less thin-skinned.

We have learned that: Dictatorships don't work in community. Some groups have failed after a period of time, because of a dominant member who becomes ill or leaves. School groups often fail, because the administration won't let them regulate themselves. Oversight takes away the fun of trying to run a responsible group website.

We have learned that: Guidelines work better than hard-and-fast rules.

We have learned that: Group members can learn a lot from one another, but many tend to be insatiable. They want to learn HTML. They want in-depth critiques of their writing. Enlisting technology and journalism professionals to provide mentoring from time to time raises the level of quality in the group. Working or retired professionals are willing to help in their spare time or participate more fully if they are retired.

We have learned that: Many groups like to have a sense of the numbers of readers. Unless they pay for it, precise numbers are hard to come by, but groups such as Stat Counter and Google Analytics are set up to give you enough page view and hits data on a day-by-day basis to convey trends in readership.

We have learned that: Readers need reminders. Unless a site has RSS feeds – which we recommend – even a loyal reader, going about his or her life, may not be compelled to check out your site. Members need to be pro-active about promoting their site. Two devices that help are listservs and plain old email. Some publications put together a listserv based on the input of email addresses from all the members. Someone writes a summary of what the current site features and out it goes to hundreds of recipients. The Junior Journal, Melrose Mirror and Rye Reflections choose a more personal approach. Each member sends a notice to his or her own list with a personalized message. It seems more intimate. Alert reporters who write about an institution might be able to convince that institution to send out an alert to its members. A Rye Reflections reporter did that after writing a story about a golf course. He asked the golf pro if a note be sent out to members and more than 300 hits on the story were recorded in the next two days.

The Rye group also makes up 8 ½ x 11 posters – the front page with a URL in large type on the top – that it posts in public buildings, a coffee shops, at the Recycling Center, in a busy blood lab waiting room, etc. Calling cards and bookmarks with the URL and pertinent information are also given out. And the Rye Public Library makes two hard copies of each page of *Rye Reflections* for those who don't have computers. One copy can be checked out like a book.

We have learned that: Being published on a group website enhances self-esteem. "My working on the Satterlights has given me the confidence to try new ventures as part of life's great adventure," Elaine Pitler once wrote. The Satterlights are a small group of residents from a retirement home called the Jack Satter House on the oceanfront of Revere, Mass.

We have learned that: No two group websites are the same. Even when they have modeled themselves after other sites, they take on their own personality. The Melrose Mirror is hyperlocal and rich with nostalgia. A site called Mummon Kammari in

Finland patterned itself after Melrose with encouragement from a MIT Media Lab student, but its bent is more toward storytelling. The Satterlights run a lot of stories about the sea and about the members' Jewish heritage. Rye Reflections stretches its coverage beyond the town borders to include the 17-mile New Hampshire Seacoast region and the nine Isles of Shoals a few miles off Rye's shore. The Junior Journal spoke loudly and clearly about issues and concerns and the culture of young people.

Sea scenes are a favorite among Rye Reflections' readers. (Photo by Judy Underwood)

We have learned that: Regular meetings are as important as the reporting, picture taking and publishing. That's where idea sharing, learning, critiquing of one another's work, policy making and planning ahead take place. Rye opens its meetings by giving each attendee a chance to share something irrelevant to the publication (a new website they've found, a pleasant family experience, feedback they've received from readers, a new technology trick they've learned . . .). Meetings, if weekly, should be held on the same day and at the same time so that they become part of the participant's routine. Rotating of the chairperson role and minutes-taker are desirable to get everyone involved and to share the burden. A typed agenda, usually prepared by the chairperson, keeps everyone on the same "page" and makes meetings more efficient. Prolonged technical discussions can be a bore for some. If a lengthy discussion is needed on how to write code for tables with three legs, it should be put off till after the meeting for those interested. It's ideal to have a computer connected to a projector with either a screen or a blank wall for "show and tell".

We have learned that: As bureaucratic as it may sound, a mission statement is worth crafting. Waiting six months after starting may make the exercise more meaningful. By that time the group has a better sense of self. For that matter a mission statement can be rewritten any time along the way. Is it necessary to frame a set of goals? No, but goals can prevent getting stuck in a rut. They can challenge a group to reach higher.

We have learned that: There's no end to learning.

CHAPTER TWELVE

The Future

"We should be able to not only interact with other people but also to create with other people."

Sir Timothy Berners-Lee, 1999 [1]

THE RITUAL OF the String occurred monthly, usually on the first business day. As soon as The Editor saw me enter the front door of the newspaper carrying my notebook, she would reach into the drawer under the reception desk and pull out the string. It wasn't just any string.

At age 16 I was sports correspondent for a small city weekly, the *Melrose Free Press*. My pay was based on the number of inches of clippings that I had pasted into my scrapbook during the month. The Editor measured the stories with a string that was 21 inches long, the length of a column of type. This ritual process accounts for why correspondents became known as "stringers". My rate was 10 cents an inch (no, I wasn't a tight writer in those days). Meanwhile, I also was a sports stringer for the Boston Globe, Boston Herald-Traveler, Boston Post and Boston Record-American-Advertiser. Among them the Boston newspapers added up to seven dailies and four Sunday publications.

Use of a string for measuring originated in the composing rooms of newspapers. Compositors always had a string hanging from their belts or scrunched up in their pocket. When there was a hole in the page form that held the metal type, out would come the string. The compositor (also called printer) would measure the opening, then go looking for a story that would fit that length.

Today editors and designers draw layouts designating where each and every story goes, mapping them onto a large computer screen. In some systems, a press of a button transmits the page to the pressroom.

Use of news, sports and college stringers was part of basic operating procedure for daily newspapers until about 40 years ago when newsroom budget cutting came into vogue, and metropolitan newspapers turned more toward stories about trends and issues and less toward breaking news.

Newspapers up until then would have a stringer in every city and town to cover events and live news. Often those stringers worked fulltime for weeklies; thus the fees paid for spot coverage were paltry since the stringers already were being paid.

The string has fallen into disuse, but the word "stringers" continues with a certain nostalgic ring. Little did I know that 50 years later I would be working with a new form of "stringers" in the same city, about a quarter mile down the street at a senior center in Melrose, Mass.

Mainstream Media Faces Sudden Shift

The Melrose Free Press, which celebrated its 100th anniversary in 2001, is a small, local example of what's happening to the mainstream media in the U.S. A gray, single-story building around the corner from Main Street housed the entire operation in this city of 30,000 in Massachusetts when I started there in 1950. The front door was at the edge of the sidewalk, and a small lobby with a counter welcomed those delivering wedding notices or press releases or advertising or whatever. Up close and personal.

Now there is no building. The Free Press staff operates four towns away (a distance of 13 miles or just under a half hour by car), having been moved when the *Free Press* became part of a chain of more than 100 newspapers put together by Fidelity in the late 1900's.

First-hand reporting and spontaneous stories that result from rubbing elbows with citizens and officials are fast fading. Media entities, large and small, have precious few reporters on the ground, getting the smell of the greasepaint and hearing the roar of the crowd.

What the Future Holds

The cover photo on farewell edition of Junior Journal, still accessible online.
(Photo by Spiros Tzelepsis)

As groups proliferate, the possibilities for synergies will evolve. Logic would suggest the following differing scenarios:

1. Community groups, especially those who refrain from the use of advertising, will remain independent.
2. Community groups will link in a variety of ways with mainstream media.
3. Community groups will link with one another.

Independent Community Groups

Those who see community publishing as a hobby and a cause are likely to maintain their independence. It's simpler. You don't have to be beholden to anyone. It's like being part of a Discussion Club or Book Club. You enjoy writing or taking photographs. You enjoy dabbling in technology. You enjoy the camaraderie. Commercial community websites are not that much different except that deriving all or part of one's livelihood becomes part of the motivation.

Mainstream Media, Community Linkage

A fire breaks out at 4 in the morning. A newspaper or other media outlet needs to get a reporter and photographer there fast. Down the street lives a member of a community publishing group. A quick phone call does the job.

Or, in a more likely scenario, a Town Council meeting is scheduled to take up an important issue. No staff person is available, often the case in stretched-thin newsrooms these days. A citizen "stringer" is asked to cover it.

A non-profit website, ChiTownDailyNews.org. won a Knight Foundation News Challenge grant in 2007 with just this approach in mind. It described its project as attempting to "recruit and train a network of 75 citizen journalists – one in each Chicago neighborhood. The journalists will work with editors to produce a professional, comprehensive daily local news report." ChiTown employs trained reporters as well. No reason why newspapers cannot do likewise.

Richmond, Virginia, is ready-made for such a set-up. In 2008 that city had 10 neighborhood news sites among a total of 16 community-journalism sites of various kinds.

Linking with One Another

Networking of community publishing groups would seem inevitable. The concept and technology steps to achieve a community of communities are spelled out in an MIT doctoral thesis by Marko Turpeinen of Finland, written in 2000.

Turpeinen proposed a grassroots newswire system "designed to build bridges across community boundaries by comparing the works of groups and by introducing members of these groups to each other electronically." Sort of a Community Facebook.

Operating on the basis that communities, like individuals, have personalities of their own, Turpeinen created a tool to collect information from groups and develop models that would be based on the contents and style of their publications, interests, geography, history and publishing practices.

Turpeinen had worked with numerous community-publishing groups and saw the potential for exchanging story ideas, page layout concepts and publishing practices. He envisioned groups acting as mentors for one another, especially in the case of experienced groups helping startups.

He also proposed a shared dynamic database that would enable a person writing a story about hurricanes (his example) to find out what other groups had written on the subject and possibly get ideas about resources, history, writing approaches, graphics, etc.

Power of Positive Thinking

The thesis, entitled "Enabling, Modeling and Interconnecting Active Community Publishers," brings us back to Marilyn Ferguson's theme in her book "Aquarian Conspiracy". She forecast that the emergence of groups around topics would become a strong phenomenon. News is a topic. Further, Ferguson hypothesized, these groups would start to link (a did the Physicians Against Nuclear War, to name one).

Indeed, she wrote, groups of varying types would become a more positive force than governments. Community publishing groups can be a part of that aquarian conspiracy and – once they start connecting and feeding off each other – will become a powerful, positive force as well.

ENDNOTES

Introduction:

1   The newspaper publishing process had remained essentially unchanged from the time Johann Gutenberg introduced the printing press in 1450. Guglielmo Marconi's demonstration of wireless telegraph more than 100 years ago is often credited with pioneering radio, but the U.S. Supreme Court in 1943 decided that the real founder of modern radio was Nicola Tesla of Croatia. In either case, radio, principally using AM and FM bands, has been doing about the same things for a century (Would you believe that 50 years ago my typewritten stories as a United Press sportswriter covering the Celtics at Boston Garden were relayed to my bureau by a Morse Code operator?). Meanwhile, the first television patent was granted in 1927. Within a few years RCA, Westinghouse and General Electric pooled efforts to develop commercial TV. The first network began in 1946, followed almost 30 years later by cable, color and satellite.

2   Editor & Publisher magazine, January 24, 1998.

Chapter Two:

1.   Interviewed in Modern Maturity Magazine (AARP publication), March/April 2002 edition.

2.   Varrell, William M. Jr., "Rye on the Rocks", Marcus Press, Boston 1962 (second printing), Pages 105-110.

3. "Cyberville: Clicks, Culture and the Creation of an Online Town," published by Warner Books Inc., January 1, 1998.
4. Melrose Mirror (http://melrosemirror.media.mit.edu), article entitled "Looking Back," by Arnold Koch, October 21, 2004.

Chapter Three:

1. Here is the wording used:

INFORMATION NOTICE

Unless indicated otherwise, the copyright for articles and other works published in Rye Reflections belongs to the individual authors or contributors. Readers may freely download and/or print pages, data or other materials on the website for personal or classroom use, provided there is a proper copyright notice and credit is given to the author or co-authors of the material copied. However, for any other intended uses, you must obtain written permission from the copyright owner. You can click on "Write to us!" on the first page to request such permission.

The software for this website is licensed to the Melrose Mirror by the Massachusetts Institute of Technology ("MIT").

Opinions expressed in Rye Reflections are solely those of the individual authors and do not reflect the views of the sponsoring Rye Senior SERVE organization, Massachusetts Institute of Technology ("MIT"), or any supporting organizations.

"Letters to the Editor" shall become the property of the Rye Reflections and may be published, when specified, using your first name only, your city or town and country. Full names would be preferred.

Chapter Twelve:

1. Berners-Lee, T. (1999) Weaving the Web: The Original Design and Ultimate Destiny of the World Wide Web by Its Inventor, HarperCollins, New York.

APPENDIX

What follows are at-a-glance tutorials on the topics of research, reporting, interviewing, writing, revision, editing, photography, idea development and journalistic issues.

RESEARCH

BASIC TOOLS – A pen or pencil and paper. Good enough? Veteran reporters prefer pens and usually carry two, in case the first one runs out of ink. If you use a pencil, carry at least two. Lead breaks easily. Spiral notebooks that fit in your hand or are a little larger and can fit in your pocket or in a purse are practical. Another technique is to fold a piece or paper (or two pieces) into a size small enough to fit into your hand for ease of taking notes. Be sure to number each page.

Research is an important part of reporting.

Research is an important part of reporting. For most stories it is the first step. Before going out to report on an event or do an interview, do as much preparation as possible. Research is a form of searching. Ask yourself the question: "What am I looking for?" You would never go on a search without knowing why you are wandering through the woods. You do so, because your dog is lost or you want to gather wild flowers. The same is true of research: Be as clear in your mind as you can about what you are trying to find. Write it down. Otherwise you will waste a lot of time wandering.

Decide where you wish to look.

Decide where you wish to look. Think of yourself as an explorer. The more sources of reliable information you can find the better: a library, which has books, newspapers, magazines and other materials; websites on the internet; certain government offices where records are kept; people who are experts on the topic What motivates an explorer is the prospect of discovery. It's an exciting feeling to dig up information that clicks. Often you will hit dead ends before you reach that moment of discovery, but bear in mind that exhaustive research, which you should strive for, can be exhausting.

Notes save you the trouble of memorizing.

It is pretty impossible to do research without taking notes that you write on paper or type into your computer. Notes save you the trouble of memorizing. They save you from looking up a piece of information a second time at a later date. They also help you absorb the information in your mind. It is better to have too many notes than too few. One technique is take careful handwritten notes, then type them when time permits. You might wish to organize notes by subject matter. Retyping gives you a better grasp of the material you have gathered. Well-organized research notes translate into easier writing in the end.

Make note when you are taking notes.

Make note when you are taking notes. Note the name of the book; jot down the name of the publisher and author or authors, the year of publication, what page your notes are taken from. If necessary, make note of any footnotes as well.

If your source is a magazine or newspaper, note the official name (is it *The London Times* or the *Times of London*; is it *New York Times* or *The New York Times*); note the author, the date of publication, the page number(s).

Be especially careful when researching website material, because the information frequently comes from another source. Clicking on links sometimes leads to the original material. Some web stories list references at the bottom of their stories.

Where do I begin?

Let's say you pick up a textbook with a title something like, "The History of the World". It has more than 1000 pages. It would make a good doorstop. You stare at it and finally say to yourself, "Where do I begin?"

Rather than start at Page 1 and read the entire book, what you want to do is look for clues. The best clues are in the front and in the back of the book. Something called The Table of Contents usually is found in the front and contains chapter titles. In the back is the Index, an alphabetical listing of names and words with page references. In some books the Index is thorough; other books only list important names and words. In either case the Index can send you right to the pages you most need to look at.

Photographs often provide valuable clues, too. Sometimes there is a listing of photos in the front of the book with page numbers. Sometimes books are printed with the photos all clustered together on successive pages. At worst, you might have to flip through the pages to find pictures connected to your research. Occasionally the photographs will lead you to significant information because of what they depict or what is mentioned in the caption or because of some information you get visually from the photo.

How best to use search engines?

Internet search engines are like double-edged swords. They are easy to use but contain the most inaccurate information. It's best to have at least two sources for information that is taken from the internet, making sure one isn't copying from the other.

Take the time to study how best to use these search engines. Sometimes the best results come when you use the fewest words in your search query. An owner of one of the biggest sites has said that three search words get the best results from his search engine.

Use quotation marks around words or phrases that are exactly what you are looking for, such as a name or a phrase. "Old King Cole" without quotes may retrieve more references to Nat King Cole, a popular 20th Century singer, than to the merry old soul.

Take the time to familiarize yourself with the tricks of the search-engine trade. Most have similar rules, but some have tricks or shortcuts that speed your research.

Human beings sometimes are fountains of information.

Research doesn't always have to entail pouring through drawers of file-cabinet folders with moths flying out or slogging through a half dozen thick encyclopedias.

Human beings sometimes are fountains of information that may never find its way into a library: The 85-year-old who could tell what the Great Depression was like in about 20 states, because he was a hobo; the Irish wood carver whose intricate designs were passed down from his County Meath ancestors; the nurse who worked with Mother Theresa in India; the botanist, the butcher, the baker. Humans enjoy talking about what they are good at or about subjects they have expertise with.

If you have access to a tape recorder, ask the person you are interviewing for permission to record what is said. But you should still take notes as best you can for two reasons: (1) it will help you find important quotes on the tape when you are organizing in preparation for writing; (2) the tape recorder might fail to work!

When in doubt, check it out.

We have established that a researcher is a good advance planner, an explorer, a collector and a keeper of notes and an organizer. We also have suggested that good note taking avoids the need to look up a piece of information a second time.

However, bear in mind that second checking is often a plus and never a minus. The ultimate aim is accuracy. You may be able to remember what year the War of 1812 started, but do you know when the Peloponnesian War began and ended? If you are unsure, even if you looked it up once, double check it.

Editors frequently spout the following: When in doubt, check it out.

Never guess!

The need for accuracy cannot be overemphasized. So what causes inaccuracies? Generally the original mistake is made in the research phase and copied in the writing phase. If you jot down a wrong date in your notes, it's likely to inaccurate when you write.

Care should be taken when it comes to bits of information: the spelling of a name or a person's middle name, a date, a geographic location, a person's exact title, etc. Be especially careful that you correctly spell the main subject of your research.

Usually a second reference can be used as a double check on factoids: an encyclopedia, a dictionary, an atlas or book of maps, even a telephone book. When in doubt, check it out.

According to whom?

Certain information is common knowledge: The Earth is round, airplanes fly; horses have four legs. Other information is less obvious or may even be controversial (only a few hundred years ago many believed the Earth was flat). Be sure to make note of the source of your information when taking notes on less obvious or controversial facts.

Not only does the name of the original source add to accuracy but it also helps the reader judge whether the information is believable.

Be as accurate as humanly possible.

As efficient as we may be, we often have to do research on our research.

When it comes time to write, we look at our notes and frequently question whether they are thorough enough or even whether they are totally accurate. After doing a lot of research on a subject, we sometimes find that little inconsistencies in our own early notes sometimes jump out at us.

It's time to re-research. Even the best researchers at times end up going back to the library or to the web to double-check certain items. Never hesitate, because you want what you ultimately write to be as accurate as humanly possible.

Double-checking is not a sign of weakness; it is a sign of strength and wisdom.

Separate the wheat from the chaff.

You've finished your research, and you've got all this material piled high. Now what?

Assumedly you have organized your notes in the course of your research, putting apples in one pile, oranges in another and pears in another. Still, you'll usually find you have too much information. This is a plus.

One way to determine what's important is to start writing without looking at your notes. Write from memory. Do a fast draft. What's most important will pop into your mind. Then go back to your research notes and get the exact date, the exact quote or whatever. As you are browsing, you may also stumble across some additional facts you had forgotten about.

Grain farmers refer to this process as "separating the wheat from the chaff." For you that should mean identifying what information in your notes is important and what is fluff.

REPORTING

Swimming alone is not a good idea.

Two heads are better than one. Three are better still. Rather than plunge into the reporting, it's a good idea to take a short time to plan your reporting strategy. Sitting down with one or more other persons and brainstorming is a valuable technique. What is the main point of the story you are reporting on? Where can you go to find out the most about it? Who are the best people to talk with? In what order? It like swimming in a river: You don't want to just jump in without thinking. You want to find the best spot, where it's not too shallow and not too deep; where boats are unlikely to be buzzing around; where the current is right; where others are nearby (swimming alone is not a good idea).

Even a few minutes spent sharing ideas with a parent, a brother or sister, another student, a teacher or a librarian will save wasting a lot of time in the end.

Take note of your surroundings.

Your story should deliver to the reader more than just the facts you collect. Words are symbols. You use them to convey to the reader what you've seen, felt, heard, smelled and, yes, maybe even tasted.

A television camera allows the audience to see and hear what the photojournalist chooses to shoot. Word pictures often can go beyond pictures, revealing what the camera might not be able to focus on; describing feelings ("the doorknob was so cold that the skin of your fingers stuck to it") and aromas ("as you walked through the Italian section, the smell of pizza baking made your mouth water").

The smallest detail sometimes speaks volumes.

A court stenographer records everything that is said during a trial; a reporter takes notes on the important questions and answers but at the same time is aware of details that may or may not have anything to do with what is being said.

When you are interviewing someone, details also can be more revealing than the words that are spoken. Let's say the health teacher tells you she is announcing a school campaign to promote better eating. On the same day you see the teacher leaving the cafeteria with a pile of French fries, a slice of cake, and an extra-large soda on her tray.

The above example is only in jest, just to help make the point, which is: No matter what type of story is being reported, the smallest detail sometimes speaks volumes to the reader.

Two is better than one; three is better still.

A veteran editor told his staff again and again: You must engage in over-reporting.

He knew the value of details. And he knew the value of corroborating information.

If one person tells you that the mayor likes to make phone calls for an hour early every morning, is that enough corroboration? Having two sources for that information is better; having three is best. Verifying this information through the mayor is ideal. The more important and sensitive the information is the more sources are needed. Over-reporting is the only way to be sure. (When you have more than one source, attribute your information to the most significant and credible source, such as the vice mayor rather than the city hall intern.)

Take notes on top of your notes.

Accuracy results from careful, meticulous reporting. Errors result from failure to keep good notes of what you see and hear. Errors can also result from bias. So always avoid inserting your own opinion into what you report.

Here's a tip: Take notes on top of your notes.

What does that mean? Reporters often find a quiet corner after completing an interview or after covering an event. There they huddle with head down, feverishly writing in their notebook while their memory is still fresh.

They might find certain quotations in their notes that lack a word or two due to haste. Or they may wish to jot down certain observations that are still clear in their mind, such as the color of a dress, the number of people in a room, the make and model of an automobile that might be part of the story. From experience they know they may not remember some of these points when it's time to write.

Few of us have a photographic memory. Time tends to make memory murky. Notes that build on notes can produce near-photographic results.

Credibility is key.

"To err is human." If Alexander Pope hadn't written that, we would all have a guilty conscience, because we all make mistakes. But we can't use that as an excuse.

If your story contains inaccuracies, it becomes less believable. Credibility is key.

Most errors occur in spelling, use of names and titles, numbers or geographic locations.

Double-checking never hurts. No one likes to be misidentified in print, so never hesitate to ask, "Could you spell your name please?" Or, "Your title is chancellor of the exchequer, correct?"

Getting the basics correct is a good start. Then you can worry about the subtleties, such as whether the actress sits straight in a chair at the table and looks you straight in the eye or slouches in a big, pillowy sofa and stares out the window during your interview.

Chew it over, then digest it.

As you gather information, stop every so often and asks, "What do all these details mean?" It is not enough to pile up fact upon fact. When you eat, you place a portion of your food in your mouth, chew it over, then digest it. It is the same with reporting.

The process is known as providing perspective.

When you are taking photographs, you often take several close-ups, then adjust your lens to get a broader view. The same is true with writing.

Another way to gain perspective is to use comparisons. If you refer to the average number of students in a classroom at your school, how does it compare with the number of students per classroom in other schools in your community or nearby?

Making comparisons in order to gain perspective often is useful when referring to amounts of money. What does it mean to say the government is spending $3 million a year on a certain type of children's program? If we can compare that figure with the amount of spending on similar programs as well as including the total annual government budget figure, it helps the reader digest the significance of all those numbers.

Face to face is best.

Asking a person questions face to face is recommended. Most people respond better in person. It also lets you get a better sense of the person. You can observe and note expressions and even hand gestures.

Email and telephone also have their place in reporting. They are especially useful if you have just a quick question or two, or if the person you wish to interview is too busy to meet with you. An advantage with email is that you can send as many questions as you wish whenever you wish. The problem is that you might not get the answers you asked for. They might be too short or are not quite a response to what you asked. You don't have the opportunity for a follow-up question the way you do when you interview in person.

The advantage of using the telephone for reporting is that you can get a quick response (assuming the person is available to take the call). The disadvantage is that people generally don't have time for a lot of phone questions. If you have more than a couple of questions, the best tactic is to call and ask for a time when you can call back. Give an estimated amount of time it will take. Here's a tip: Never ask for more than 20 minutes. You risk getting turned down altogether.

Don't believe everything you read.

Nicholas Gage was a well-known *New York Times* reporter. It is said that he got hooked on investigating/reporting while he was a Boston University student. A building on the college campus had earlier been a hotel, where the famous playwright Eugene O'Neill died. Gage read in a book that in the playwright's dying moments he turned to his wife and asked her to burn his unfinished manuscripts in the hotel room fireplace.

Gage checked the room. No fireplace. So he checked the blueprints. No plan for a fireplace. So he called the widow, who told him she gave the manuscripts to a janitor who burned them in a basement furnace. Gage called the publisher and the book was changed.

Moral: Don't believe everything you read. Indeed, don't assume any fact is true. I checked two sources before writing this Nicholas Gage anecdote.

How do you know when you are done?

How do you know when you've finished your reporting?

Well, after you've collected enough information to support your story, you should take two more steps:

1. Test the old formula sometimes known as the "5 W's and an H." The letters stood for: Who? What? When? Where? Why? And How? If you can't answer one of those questions, you undoubtedly need to do more reporting.

2. Put yourself in the place of the reader. What questions, large or small, would you want answered in the story? If you can answer those questions, then the fun is about to begin: It's time to write.

INTERVIEWING

Here are a dozen do's and don'ts:

1. Do as much research as you can before you start your interviews.
2. Decide whom you wish to interview and in what order. (Tip: The most important interviews should be done last).
3. Write out your questions ahead of time and in the order you think they should be asked and never start out with a big, important question. Ease the person into the interview in a conversational way.
4. Make an appointment to do the interview. After introducing yourself, explain briefly what story you are working on.
5. Ask all the questions you have written out but be alert. You'll find that added questions often will pop into your mind as the interview unfolds.
6. Be sure to have enough paper and pencils or pens.
7. Use a tape recorder when appropriate and ask permission to use it. Don't totally rely on the tape recorder. Be on the safe side. Take notes.
8. Be a good listener, but don't let the person you are interviewing ramble. Try to draw out specifics: How much, how long, when, etc.
9. Make mental or written notes about the person (gestures, mannerisms) and the place (color, size, decorations, furniture, etc.).
10. Exchange contact information in case either of you wishes to contact the other at a later date with new, added or corrected information.
11. Don't forget a photograph. If you are having someone else take a picture at a later time, make the arrangements at the end your interview.
12. While the interview is still fresh in your mind, go to a quiet place to review and reconstruct your notes.

WRITING

I don't know what you mean.

Writing involves having a conversation without sound.

You are conveying information to others using words that are written rather than spoken.Indeed, some good writers move their lips when they are writing. Others make believe they are writing for their favorite aunt or a good friend in an effort to remind themselves that they are writing for an audience rather than for themselves.

The advantage of the written word over the spoken word is that you have time to correct mistakes or explain something more clearly. How many times have you said to yourself, "O, I wish I hadn't said that." Or how many times has someone said to you, "I don't know what you mean."

Writing is a luxury. It gives you time to correct your "conversation" or to be better understood.

Just let it flow.

Good writing is good thinking.

Words, sentences and paragraphs are a reflection of what's on your mind. Well-known writers understand this, so they write as fast as they can, not concerning themselves with spelling, punctuation or even sentence structure, because the mind works faster than they can write or type. They can go back and fix things up later. The famous 19th Century poet and essayist Walt Whitman once said, "I just let her come till the fountain runs dry."

In the process of emptying the mind a writer sometimes uncovers a surprise in the sub-conscious. It's like cleaning the attic. You often find things you forgot were there. This element of surprise or discovery is part of the magic of writing.

So as Whitman suggests, just let it flow.

Focus

Writers start with a blank sheet but not a blank mind. With all those millions of thoughts running around in your head, how do you know what to write.

The solution: Focus.

Just as you need to adjust the lens of your camera to get a clear photograph, so too do you need to get your thoughts in focus.

Three techniques are recommended.

Novelist William Faulkner is said to have written down on a card the three or four words that best summed up the point or theme or focus of the book he was writing. He propped up the card over his typewriter and kept it always in front of him as he wrote. So that's Technique No. 1: Write down in a few words what the focus is. In fact try writing it a dozen ways until you have precisely the focus you want.

Technique No. 2 is to bear in mind that, with few exceptions, stories have a beginning, a middle and an end.

Technique No. 3 is to write an outline. It doesn't necessarily have to have Roman numerals, capital letters and all that goes with a formal outline. But it is worth jotting down the order of points you want to make in the beginning, middle and end. Then start going through your notes to figure out where they fit within the outline you've designed.

Every word has a function.

Words draw a picture in the mind of the reader. Some words add color and life; others draw a blank.

Analyze the following sentence: "Paris is interesting, but it is very hot in July." What does "interesting" mean? What is the difference between "hot" and "very hot"?

"Interesting" and "very" are weak words that should be avoided.

Another frequently useless and misused word is "different"? If you write, "We visited Mexico City on two different occasions, the sentence would benefit by dropping the word "different".

However, if you wrote, "Buenos Aires and Calcutta are different," the word "different" would provide a useful function, providing you then explained what the differences are.

Be sure that every word in every sentence has a function.

"A lightning bug and lightning"

The more you write the more you learn to write.

You learn that clarity often results from revision of what you first wrote. You learn that rhythm or flow is as important to writing as it is to music. You learn that writing is like a puff of smoke unless it is based on facts (even opinion writing is more compelling if it is based on factual information rather than on random thoughts spouted by the writer). You learn that writing is like cooking, because too much or too little of certain ingredients can ruin it. You learn the importance of word choice. When you are re-reading what you have written, the change of a word here and there can add clarity, it can enhance rhythm, it can lend authority, it can add spice to the ingredients.

Mark Twain, author of *Tom Sawyer*, once wrote, "The difference between the almost right word and the right word is the difference between a lightning bug and lightning."

Read what you have written aloud.

How can you be confident that what you write is smooth yet tightly written, clear yet vivid? Three easy techniques seem to work well.

One is to read what you have written aloud. If it sounds even the slightest bit awkward, you probably need to do some revising.

The second is to have it read critically by a friend or family member or interested person (teacher, editor, etc.).

The third requires some time. Put aside what you have written for at least an hour but preferably overnight. Then re-read it. You'll be surprised what new perspectives you will bring to what you have written.

Help the reader see, hear and feel.

Think of adjectives as being describers. They describe a noun ("The floppy rim of her hat.") or a pronoun ("He is red-headed.").

Author Thomas Wolfe was a master of description, who could write page after page about what he saw looking out the window of a train. Here's a sentence about a truck from his book, *You Can't Go Home Again*:

The heavy motor warmed up with a full-throated roar, then there was a grinding clash of gears, and George felt the old house tremble under him as the truck swung out into the street and thundered off.

His use of adjectives helps you see, hear and feel the truck.

"Unusually" is useful

Think of adverbs as being assistants to adjectives and verbs. Often but not always they end in "ly".

Adverbs add meaning to adjectives and verbs. Avoid adverbs that fail to add meaning.

Good use: "When the bell rang, she left her classroom immediately."

Weak use: "When the bell rang, she immediately remembered she needed to meet her friend."

Only use adverbs that play a useful role. Words such as "generally", "usually" or "occasionally" serve to qualify (for example: "It's usually hot in Rome in July.").

Words such as "frequently" or "forever" answer the question "When".

Getting your thoughts on paper

You've done the research. You've organized your notes, sketched out an outline and written a sentence or phrase that reflects the focus. Now what? How do you begin?

If you're not too sure, write a topic sentence and keep going from there. You can always go back and change the opening. Another approach some writers use when a good beginning fails to pop into their minds is to begin with the second paragraph and wait till they've finished before writing the first paragraph. Some write a quick draft, just to get thoughts on paper. Others put their notes aside, rather than becoming bogged down by looking back and forth. They then fill in the gaps with specifics such as dates, first names and middle initials, exact quotes and the like.

Probably the best way to start is to dash off twenty or thirty potential first sentences. Then go back and pick out the best. Lots of writers do this, because they find that they arrive at certain words and phrases that click after the first dozen attempts. In some cases they'll decide to use the best sentence in the middle of the story or as an ending.

There's no right way.

You best writing may occur away from the keyboard. When you least expect it, the exact point of the story or a special turn of a phrase might leap into your mind.

A newspaper reporter mentally writes her story while returning to the office after covering an event. A magazine writer comes to grips with writing themes while cooking dinner. A feature writer goes for a walk, head down, not noticing passersby, ideas churning with each step. A deadline writer, with the clock ticking away, leans back in his chair, feet on the edge of the desk for balance, and closes his eyes. A couple of minutes later, he sits upright and writes a flawless story from beginning to end as fast as he can type.

These are not fictional examples. They describe real people approaching the writing process differently. There's no right way; there's only your way.

A beginning, a middle and an end

Newspapers once had a theory that the most important information should go at the top of the story and the least important should go at the end. The theory was known as the "inverted pyramid". If a story needed to be shortened, it was cut from the bottom up.

Today newspapers, magazines and websites generally agree with the theory that a story should have a beginning, a middle and an end. Indeed, many believe the ending is the most important of the three, because it is what is most remembered by the reader.

Frequently writers decide how their stories will end before they determine the beginning.

The beginning and the ending should echo one another, holding together the middle, as though they were two pieces of bread in a sandwich.

Speaking of food, do you often leave the last good bite of a meal till the end? Readers of stories also like to savor that last bite of information.

REVISION

Revision is the key to improved writing

1. Revision IS writing. It's almost impossible to write a story perfectly from top to bottom on the first attempt. Don't even try. Write the first draft fast, then go back, at least once, and revise.
2. Embrace revision as a part of the writing process, whether you are writing an essay or an email message. Make it a habit. It can only improve what you write.

3. Read aloud what you have written. Listen as though it were music. If a note is off, change is in order. If it's not crystal clear, smooth out the wording.

4. It takes a while even for good writers to get used to criticism from others. Yet, when we criticize our own work, which is what revision is, it's fun.

5. What to look for: Is what you've written accurate? Is it focused? Too long, too short? Can one sentence be better than two? Have you selected the right key words?

6. If someone gave you a coin for every word you could delete without hurting the meaning, would you think harder about the function of each word? Make each and every word count.

7. The tone should be appropriate to the subject matter. Bouncy writing would not be in keeping with a story about illness.

8. In re-reading your story, does it sound like something you would write or does it sound like someone else? It's your story and should be told in a way that is most comfortable to you.

9. Look at the beginning. Is it likely to encourage a reader to continue on? Does it set an appropriate tone?

10. Look at the middle of your story. Is there enough detail to reveal the main message of the story? Are there anecdotes you might add to make your points more understandable?

11. Look at the ending. If it sounds like preaching, you probably want to change it. The ending should be like an exclamation mark at the end of a sentence.

12. One more point about endings: Bear in mind that, when the reader leaves a story, he or she will most remember the ending. Is your ending memorable?

13. Finally, are you satisfied? That's the final test. When you reach that point, the story is written.

EDITING

Get the feel of a story first

Teachers of speed-reading tell us that before reading a book we should scan the cover flaps and the table of contents, then quickly flip through the pages of the first couple of chapters.

The goal is to get a feel of the subject matter, see what names and key words pop up frequently and generally get acquainted with the text. Research shows that this technique improves reading speed.

The same goes for editing. Before making any changes, even as simple as fixing a typing error, read the story from top to bottom to familiarize yourself with the big picture.

Why editing is so important

Editing is a form of polishing, preferably using a soft cloth rather than sandpaper.

In short, it involves making sure words are spelled correctly, language is used properly, punctuation is in the right places and the facts are accurate.

Sloppiness can undermine the reader's understanding of a story and can put in question its believability.

Editing is black, white and gray

Spelling, correct word use, punctuation and accuracy are pretty specific. Generally there is a right and a wrong.

Other editing issues are more general and require judgment. Among those issues are clarity, awkwardness and focus.

Is the story clear to anyone with average intelligence? Are there sentences, clauses or phrases that would make you stumble if you read them aloud? Does the story stick to one point?

So the two roles of editing are: 1. Make right what is wrong;; 2. Use your best judgment as to whether the story is told well.

Editing may require adding

Editors are often thought of as butchers waving a meat cleaver. That description, of course, is an exaggeration, known as hyperbole.

While it is true that an editor should tighten up a story by cutting out excess words, it is also important for the editor to make sure the story is complete. Sometimes writers assume that the reader knows basic information: When World War I took place; who Mahatma Gandhi was; where Rio de Janeiro is. Use your judgment as to whether to expand on this kind of information. If you think one out of ten readers is unsure, it's better to include explanatory information.

Doughnuts have holes in the middle, but stories shouldn't. If you think more detail or description is needed, fill in the hole.

How to make a story whole

The easiest way to find holes in stories or to find other flaws that need editing is to put yourself into the mind of the reader.

What questions would the reader ask? Does the story answer those questions.

Odd as it may sound, the best editing often occurs when an editor finds something that's missing.

An easy example would be something like: "The teacher made three points." And then the story only lists two.

More difficult is the process of realizing that a piece of information necessary to make the story complete is lacking. A story with a hole cannot be whole.

Punctuation has meaning

Driving down a road you notice a variety of signs. Most signs have symbols, such as a curved arrow, meaning there's a bend in the road; some have words, such as STOP.

Punctuation in a sentence is like a sign along the road; it is intended to be helpful in guiding the reader through sentences and paragraphs. Each punctuation sign has a function. The signs are not for decoration, a dab here and a dab there.

If in editing you see a punctuation mark that performs no role, take it out. The reader, like the driver of a car, doesn't need needless distractions.

When comma goes before "and"

The comma is the most misused punctuation mark. Some writers think they should throw one in every time there is a pause in a sentence. Not true.

The word "and" seems to trigger the most problems. Examine the following two sentences:

Marguerite went to the store, and Juan rode his bike.

Marguerite went to the store and bought some yummy candy.

Note that the first example has a comma; the second doesn't. The reason? Example #1 is a compound sentence. How do you know? If you take away the word "and", you have two sentences. But in Example #2 you can't take away "and". Marguerite is the subject of "went" and "bought".

A comma is unnecessary unless it serves a specific purpose. Pause and analyze the role of each comma but don't let one be used every time there is a pause.

(How necessary are commas? Notice that only one comma is used in this tutorial).

Variations complicate editing

A close look at spelling, punctuation, capitalization and the like will reveal differences in usage between one publication and another.

Example #1

Red, white, and blue

Red, white and blue

Example #2:

Labor

Labour

In a series (Example #1) formal grammar calls for a comma before the word, and informal grammar, often found in newspapers, leaves out that comma. This practice originated because of the need for speed when type was set by hand.

"Labour" is a common British spelling used in many countries around the world.

Publishing groups develop manuals for what is known as style, because there can be so many variations. Textbooks set the style in schools.

Whether you labor or labour doesn't matter much; what's most important is that you are consistent.

Slang understood by some, not all

Slang is a form of language fashioned by those who share a special interest. Sports enthusiasts refer to the baseball field as a "diamond"; basketball players "dunk"; volleyball players "spike" the ball. Just about every profession has its own slang or lingo.

The advent of email has also brought with it a slang that is almost like a foreign language. The use of email slang is fine if the recipients understand it.

Stories on the web or in print more often than not are written for a general audience. Slang should be avoided.

By the same token obscure words, particularly those with four syllables, should also be replaced with common words, unless you are writing for an erudite audience. Erudite? It describes those who have extensive knowledge, mostly from books. Probably a good word to avoid most of the time.

Remember: It's the writer's story

Editing requires common sense, because rules cannot cover every situation. Still, any changes should be made with good reason, because the story belongs to the writer.

An improvement in the choice of a word or a phrase or a clarifying insertion or the correction of mistake are appropriate in the editing process.

What happens when substantial changes are required, such as the insertion of a paragraph or putting paragraphs in different order or reducing a story to half its original length?

In those cases the writer should be consulted. Major changes should be agreed upon between the writer and the editor before a story is published. The fine line between editing and rewriting can be dissolved by discussion and agreement.

Four elements stories should contain

Stories need to contain certain elements that make them worthwhile:

1. They should inform, educate, guide and, in some cases, entertain the reader.
2. They should be of general interest to the reader.

3. They should provide readers what they need to know or have the right to know.
4. They should contain timely information.

In short, stories should not be written for the writer but for the reader.

The last step: Read and listen

The first step and the last step in the editing process are the same: Read the story from beginning to end. When practical read it aloud. Occasionally you'll hear a bump in the story that needs smoothing.

How clear are the answers to the four basic W questions: Who? What? When? Where? Most stories also should clearly explain the How and Why as well.

Also, editors occasionally leave a stray comma here or a mistyped word there. Those need to be fixed, because this is the final polishing process. The next step is publication.

Publication is a gratifying last step that follows a long process involving the forming of an idea, researching, reporting, writing, revising and editing.

PHOTOGRAPHY

1. Understand your equipment before taking any important pictures. Read the manual. Test the camera. And, if the camera has batteries, make sure they are fresh.
2. In some cases a photo stands alone and tells a story; in other cases it goes with written words, and together they tell a story.
3. You have control over some photos you take. You choose the angle so that the sun hits properly. You decide where the subject stands. You pick the background.
4. When "shooting" a news or sports event, you have little control. The action occurs quickly. You may have no choice over the angle or framing of the photo.
5. Take general scenes and close-ups. Professionals carry more than one lens: 24mm or 28mm wide-angle or regular 50mm; 200mm for close-ups.
6. Anticipate action. Set your camera focus on an object where you guess the action might occur. Be ready to shoot quickly. You may get only one shot.
7. Carefully and accurately write down names, titles and affiliations of those you photograph. Without that information a photograph is seldom usable.
8. Group photos often present particular problems. Set up clearly defined rows. If someone is straddling two rows, the identification explanation may be awkward.

9. Posed photos generally should be avoided. Having the subject(s) engaged in normal activity makes a more natural and thus more appealing photograph.
10. Written explanations with photograph are usually called "captions" (sometimes they are called "cutlines"). The trick is to make them complete but brief.
11. Photo layouts enable in-depth storytelling. Thumbnail photographs that can be clicked on and expanded are an effective, space-saving device on web pages.
12. Slide shows should be used sparingly and only for a special reason. Web readers often are in too much of a hurry to watch them.

IDEA DEVELOPMENT

Best ideas? Yours

Stories begin with an idea. That raises the question of where ideas come from.

They can come from someone else, of course, but writers who develop their own ideas tend to execute them better. They are more enthusiastic, more inquisitive and have more of a sense of ownership (it should be quickly stated, however, that the improvement of an initial idea can best be achieved in collaboration with others: Two minds are better than one).

You arrive at a good idea by answering the following questions:

What interests you? What creates emotion: makes you mad; makes you happy/sad; makes you inquisitive?

Who interests you?

What do you want to look into more or learn about?

How good is the idea: Will it contain information? Will the information be significant enough to be of interest to others?

Capture your brainstorms

If you sit down and try to answer questions like the above, you probably will come up with some possibilities for stories to write. But generally ideas are generated more spontaneously. A brainstorm. You see, hear or read something that triggers another idea. A conversation gives you an idea.

The problem is that ideas tend to go in one ear and out the other. Ever wake up in the middle of the night with a great solution to a problem and then wake up the next morning and forget what it was?

Ideas, for many of us, are like jokes: We tend to forget them.

Most writers carry a little notebook or keep a journal. It is a way of capturing the germ of an idea that can be built on.

Putting ideas to the test

Here's another little exercise that might be worth trying: Write down three ideas you think may be interesting for your publication . . . for your eyes only.

Take your best idea. Write an answer in a word or two or three to the basic questions each story should contain, if there is an answer: Who? What? When? Where? Why? and How?

Talk over the idea with someone else before you start working on it.

What are the criteria for a newsy idea?

1. Does it have timeliness?
2. Is it of importance (affects many)?
3. Will it be of general interest to the reader?
4. Is it relevant?
5. Does it involve the public's right to know?
6. Does involve the public's need to know?
7. Will it inform/educate/guide/entertain readers?

ISSUES

Fairness

"Progress is our most important product." Those words were used as a motto for many years by General Electric. Adapting the motto to those who publish, you might say, "Fairness is our most important product."

All sides should be reflected in a story involving a controversial subject. Another well-known saying is that "there are two sides to every story." Unfortunately it is sometimes inaccurate, because many issues have more than two sides. A simple example would be a story about the proper age to get a driver's license. Some may say age 16, some 17, others 18. Others might say a license should be available only to those who need to drive at age 16 because of a job.

Even if you are writing a opinion piece, it is a good idea to summarize the positions of others. Oddly, it helps clarify your viewpoint for the reader.

Conflict of Interest

The reader deserves to know if a writer has more than a passing interest in a subject.

Surely it would be inappropriate to write a review of a play without telling your readers that you were an actor in the play. That is called having a "conflict of interest".

If you are part of an organization that you are writing a story about, you should say so in the story or in an italic line at the end of the story. Full disclosure when necessary is only being fair to the reader who otherwise would assume you had no connection.

Attribution

A favorite expression of little children is, "Says who?" Big sister says, "It's time to go to bed." The child responds, "Says who?" Actually it's a pretty smart statement. The sister doesn't have the authority to determine bedtime unless she is told to do so by a parent.

If a reader stops in the middle of the story and thinks, "Says who?", the writer and editor have failed to do their jobs properly. The story needs to state where information comes from. We call this attribution.

Common knowledge needs no attribution (the sun rises in the East); nor does a description of something you witnessed with your own eyes (the car turned left on Main Street).

When passing on what we have learned during research or reporting, we should tell where the information came from. It's best to include the "Says who?" in the same sentence that contains the information, often at the end. An easy way to do so is to add a comma and write, "according to . . . "

Linking

Links are an effective way to give attribution if you are writing for the web. By enabling a reader to click on a word or set of words to go to a source, you are "giving credit".

Whether the story is on the web or on paper, another common device is to provide a citation at the bottom of the story, saying something like, "Material in this story came from . . ." List the sources and page numbers when you can, somewhat as you might do when using footnotes at the end of a report or an essay.

Giving credit is not only being honest but it also lends authority to whatever you attribute.

Quotations

Quotations obviously need to be attributed to whoever said or wrote the words.

If you are using quotations based on an interview, there is no limit to the number of words you can use. If you are using quotes from another publication, there is a limit, known as "fair use". It's fair to use a certain amount of direct quotations that have been published elsewhere, but extensive use requires written permission from the publisher.

Copyright laws, which are similar from country to country, protect the original author from having too much of his or her work quoted without permission.

My rule of thumb is that the use of about 50 words of a direct quotation, is fair use. That, of course, assumes you give credit.

Direct, indirect quotations

Newspapers and websites sometimes run full texts of important speeches. The story that accompanies the text reports some of what is said but not all of it.

Two devices are used in stories to summarize interviews and speeches without using every word.

One device involves selecting the best quotes. If it doesn't alter the meaning of the speaker, some quoted sentences can be shortened. However, if words are omitted in the middle or end of a sentence, three periods, known as ellipses, should be inserted to signal to the reader that part of the quote has been taken out.

As an example, using the last sentence: "However . . . three periods should be inserted to signal to the reader that part of the quote has been taken out."

A second device is the use of an indirect quotation. As the writer, you use your own words to summarize what a person said. This is especially useful when someone says something important but the quote is too long or not too interesting. When writing indirect quotes, you still need to attribute. Most stories rely on a combination of direct and indirect quotations.

Reprints

Use of photographs published somewhere else, whether on a website or in print, requires written permission from the "owner".

It is not permissible to just give credit. Permission must be obtained in writing. In fact, you might have to pay a fee in some cases. When written permission is necessary, email is adequate if the owner agrees. Be sure to keep a copy in your file.

Plagiarism, fabrication

We all hold up honesty as an ideal. Some writers occasionally slip up.

The two most dishonest acts in writing are plagiarism and fabrication.

Using someone else's work or words and passing them off as yours is called "plagiarism." It's a no-no.

Fabrication occurs when you simply make up facts or quotations out of thin air. One of the worst cases I ever heard of had to do with a quote from Voltaire, an 18th Century philosopher-writer. Perhaps you've heard the quote:

"I may disagree with what you have to say, but I shall defend, to the death, your right to say it."

Trouble is, he never said it. Someone made it up and attributed it to Voltaire. We can defend a person who says something we disagree with, but we cannot defend a person who makes up quotes out of thin air.

Credibility

Why should the reader believe what we write? Believability has to be earned.

We earn believability or credibility through accuracy, through documented information, through fairness, through projecting a sense of caring, through consistency and through dependability. Believability has to be earned over time.

We need to realize the root of the word "publication". It derives from "public". And credibility in a story derives from being public-oriented.

Credit

Occasionally more than one person works on the reporting and/or writing of a story. Who gets the credit? No rulebook exists to provide the answer.

However, there is what is called the "rule of thumb". When two persons do a substantial amount of work on a story, both should get a byline, even though one might do more work than the other; that is, their names should be at the top of the story preceded by the word "by".

If someone contributes to the reporting, that person should be given credit at the bottom of the story. Usually the credit line is in italics or in parentheses.

Editors traditionally get no credit.

INDEX

J

K

L

M

N